# the tree
# that talked

Jenny Smedley

Winchester, UK
Washington, USA

First published by O Books, 2007
O Books is an imprint of John Hunt Publishing Ltd.,
The Bothy, Deershot Lodge, Park Lane, Ropley, Hants, SO24 0BE, UK
office1@o-books.net
www.o-books.net

Distribution in:

UK and Europe
Orca Book Services
orders@orcabookservices.co.uk
Tel: 01202 665432 Fax: 01202 666219 Int. code (44)

USA and Canada
NBN
custserv@nbnbooks.com
Tel: 1 800 462 6420 Fax: 1 800 338 4550

Australia and New Zealand
Brumby Books
sales@brumbybooks.com.au
Tel: 61 3 9761 5535 Fax: 61 3 9761 7095

Far East (offices in Singapore, Thailand, Hong Kong, Taiwan)
Pansing Distribution Pte Ltd
kemal@pansing.com
Tel: 65 6319 9939 Fax: 65 6462 5761

South Africa
Alternative Books
altbook@peterhyde.co.za
Tel: 021 447 5300 Fax: 021 447 1430

Text copyright Jenny Smedley 2007

Design: Stuart Davies

ISBN-13: 978 1 846940 35 4
ISBN-10: 1 846940 35 4

A CIP catalogue record for this book is available from the British Library.

Printed in the UK by Ashford Colour Press

# the tree that talked

Jenny Smedley

BOOKS

Winchester, UK
Washington, USA

# THE TREE THAT TALKED
# Jenny Smedley

Have you ever stood beneath a majestic 300 year old oak tree and thought, *this tree lived before I was born, and will be alive long after I am dead?*

Have you ever wondered about what such a tree might have witnessed during its long life, and thought, *if it could talk, what wonders and insight could it teach me?*

This is the story of an oak tree, from birth to death, and using the tree as our witness, we see many small moments in history - moments that rippled outwards to affect the world. We share intimate family moments, and tragedies that take place in the shade of the mighty oak.

From their conversations and actions we learn about the private lives and thoughts of those who pass by, and we understand that compared to the tree, we humans are merely transient. We scurry through our lives, rushing to the end like lemmings, often only to have to start all over again. Compared to the tree's our lives can very often appear insignificant. The tree just lives, experiences, and accepts.

It is said that a soul is like an acorn, starting out small and defenceless, and hopefully growing into a mighty oak.

Trees take very little and give a lot; man gives very little and takes as much as he can.

Who is to say that if the soul of a tree one day becomes that of a man, whether this is evolution or devolution?

Every living thing has a spirit, and we used to know that. If man accepted it again, how differently might he treat a tree?

*The talking oak to the ancient spoke*
*but any tree will talk to me*
Mary Carolyn Davies

*The wonder is that we can see these trees and not wonder more.*
Ralph Waldo Emerson

*Trees are sanctuaries. Whoever knows how to speak to them,*
*whoever knows how to listen to them, can learn the truth. They do*
*not preach learning and precepts, they preach undeterred by par-*
*ticulars, the ancient law of life.*
Hermann Hesse

# Contents

# Prologue

It was a frigid, twilight hour in 506 AD. The air was hard and icy, and frost had painted the undergrowth and trees with a sparkling white coat. Among the patchwork of growing shadows and emerging starlight reflected from the frost, a group of twenty cloaked figures followed the well-marked trail up the slight hill to a sacred tree grove at the top. Their feet made soft crunching noises as they trod over the crispy ground, and that was the only sound to be heard. They stopped at the grove entrance and the air was totally still, and their breath, as it cascaded white and smoky from their mouths, was the only movement.

No streetlights or car lights tainted the rapidly darkening sky as it moved above the group; slowly turning from dusky blue to a shade so dark it might have been black. The narrow crescent moon in this sky was so low that it seemed as if it could be touched, and it shone like a pale reflection of the now totally submerged sun. The stars gradually blossomed fully in the black, and even they were scintillating in the pure dark, despite the natural lamplight of the moon, riding with them.

The people who made up the tribe called themselves 'Son of the Yew', and they were making their way to their sacred grove of yew trees, as they had done many times before. To them the spirits of the trees were the most powerful among all the shades that dwelt in all natural things. Everything that breathed or moved on the Earth contained a soul. Even the rocks and the soil contained a conscious link to the global soul. Something as beautiful and as useful as a tree was bound to possess an especially potent soul. The yew tree in particular represented death, but it also represented rebirth and reincarnation, so it was a natural emblem of everlasting life. Not one person among them would ever have felled a tree without asking its permission first and then begging its forgiveness for having to do so. Even a fallen branch would be revered, and the tree would be thanked for providing it.

In those days of Animism, humans were seen as just one of the beings that possessed a soul or spirit, no better than any other, and worse than many. The people also believed that souls or spirits could transfer from living being to living being, in any combination. A soul could move from a plant to a plant, a tree to an animal, a river to a bird, or a human to a tree or vice versa. For, at the end of the day, all things were spiritually connected as part of the whole soul of the planet, and the same energy ran like a river through everything. The people of the time were at one with nature, and walked in step with the spiritual world, able to reach out at touch it quite naturally, whereas in the modern world we have to struggle to make any connection at all. In the modern day the natural sacredness of our planet has become all but inaccessible to humans, and yet if we did but remember, in reality we are always just one, lateral, step away.

To these people the planet had a communal soul, made up of all the living things that walked and flowed and grew upon it. Therefore by communicating with a tree, one facet of the whole, they could communicate with and join with, the whole Earth. The moment of their death was a precious opportunity for the departing soul to reunite itself with the communal soul of the Earth, through a tree, and it could thereby be immortal.

The trees of the grove were quite young saplings, but they had grown apparently naturally in an almost perfect circle, evenly spaced. They grew in the same places that other trees had grown, lived, and died before. As they had approached the circle, the people had not uttered any sounds that could be heard by a human ear, but vibrations and disturbances in the previously motionless air announced their imminent arrival to the young trees.

The people walked on in solemn procession, heads down. At the front walked two young men, a seat slung between them. On the seat rode a very elderly man, who was called Gildas (meaning serves God). Gildas was stooped and frail-looking, leaning on one of the young carriers for support; else he would have toppled from his perch. There was a head-dress made of antlers balanced on his head, and his other clothes, like the rest of the group's, were made of roughly sewn-together animal skins. The head-dress was weighing the elder down in his weakness, keeping his head bowed and his shoulders stooped as he rode onwards.

The people continued into the inner circle, and the old man was placed reverently on the ground, next to the biggest of the young yew trees, and he leaned back against the trunk. Gildas was having trouble breathing, and the group waited patiently, standing in a half-circle around him. His breathing gradually slowed, but it still rasped in his throat. With effort he removed the antlers from his head, and raised them in shaking hands, holding them out towards the rest of his tribe. Then he placed the headdress carefully on the frosty ground at his own feet.

The people of the tribe exchanged meaningful and questioning glances with each other. All eyes, including the old man's, eventually settled on a young woman expectantly. Her clothes were a little different from the rest, setting her slightly apart. Over her animal-skin clothes she wore a woven cloak covered in feathers and beads. She also stood out because the others were all dark with swarthy skins, whereas she was blond with a pale, Scandinavian cast to her complexion. She was slender and delicate. Her long, almost white hair was braided in a long plait that hung down her back. Her eyes were large and blue, and she was about fifteen years old.

Oriana was her name, (meaning blond), and her birth had been a wondrous occasion to her people, because she had been born to be a Priestess. Oriana was also thought by her people to be a direct descendant of the Goddess Brigid, daughter of Dagda, the 'good God'. In fact Oriana was really a direct descendant from the Viking pirate invaders, who had come in their Nydam boats and ravaged the countryside. She was the only surviving line in the village. Whatever her birth, her colouring had made her stand out, and this alone was reason for the tribe to believe that she was endowed with special powers.

Oriana had therefore carried a heavy burden all her life. A female, it was not fitting that she should actually rule, so the leader at the time of her birth had decreed that she should choose the new rulers on the death of the old ones. He believed she would do so wisely. At this time of his death, the elder who had chosen her was happy to leave the decision of his successor in her hands, even though by then she had been only five years old. Because the leaders were always chosen from the oldest men of the tribe, their rule did not last long, sometimes only months, before they passed to spirit. And so for ten years Oriana had been the selector of the next leader. She had already chosen two new leaders. This would be her third.

She turned round and round, facing each person in the semi-circle, considering each one carefully before moving on, and finally pointed at one man, called Druce (meaning wise). Druce nodded his head in acceptance, and then walked to the old man where he lay prone, having sunk back in exhaustion, barely conscious. Druce had been waiting all his life for this chance, and he was happy, but he was also ready to mourn the loss of Gildas, and stepping into his 'Father's' place was going to be a huge task. Druce stood beside the elder, and waited patiently, as he had been waiting for years, passed over on previous occasions because he had been too young.

Oriana followed him and knelt beside Gildas, taking his hand in hers. She placed her other hand on his grey-haired head, saying, "Father, go now, you have done all you needed to. We release you. Let your body sleep now, while your spirit walks with the stars. You have earned the right to be free. We ask that you take our messages and prayers with you on your journey to the Goddess."

The rest of the tribe began a slow chant, which steadily rose in volume and tempo. One at a time, each tribe member approached the prone elder, and pressed a feather, or a bead, or a scrap of wood into his shaking hands. Each token represented a message or plea that was to be taken to the Goddess by the old man when he passed into Spirit. He took each item respectfully, and as they handed the tokens to him, each person bowed low, and kissed the old man on the forehead, before re-taking their place in the circle. Once everyone had handed over their messages, Oriana and Druce took the scraps one by one from the old man's hands and hung them on the yew tree's lower branches. Tatters of messages from previous ceremonies still clung there, turned ragged by the wind through the years.

Oriana placed both her hands on the trunk of the largest tree, above the elder's bowed head. Her fingers caressed the smooth, golden brown bark as she spoke. "Tree spirit, take our Father, Gildas, to your heart and bear our messages with him. Let his soul rise with your life-force, up towards the stars as you grow ever taller, until the Goddess can reach him."

The people believed that the elder's body would give back sustenance to the land that had spawned him, while his spirit would pass into the tree, bearing the messages and prayers of those still living, to the Goddess. All eyes returned to the figure of the old man as he suddenly sagged. With a slow gasp, he died, and his body gently subsided against the tree. The people immediately turned their eyes up and along the trunk of the tree as if they could see the energy of their dead leader swarming upwards through it, towards heaven and the Goddess.

After a few moments Oriana turned to Druce, her selected heir to Gildas, who still stood at her side. "May the spirit of the stag, and the soul of the tree, make you as strong a leader as our beloved Father, Gildas has been."

Druce retrieved the horned head-dress from the feet of the old man and placed it carefully and proudly upon his own head. He was already tall and still strong, and yet the placing of the head-dress seemed to make him grow bigger and more powerful. Druce was anxious, yet excited. His time had finally come to lead his people, and the old man had truly been a worthy leader. Druce gazed up at the tree again, sparing not a glance for the empty body that lay at his feet, which to him was now nothing more than a shell. The soul of Gildas had risen into the tree, and would be immortal, bonded with the tree, and from there, as one with the Earth.

"Thank you my Father," Druce said.

Oriana led the others of the tribe as they all made a low bow to each tree of the circle of seven in turn, and then they followed her away from the grove, leaving Gildas' body where it lay, so that the material part of him would give life and nourishment to the Earth.

Each one of the tribe felt safe in the knowledge that the circle of life and death and rebirth was unbroken. As they walked away, the tribe started to chant again, and this sound, gradually fading, marked their passage back down the trail. Eventually the grove was silent once more, and empty, save for the discarded body of the old man, his spirit gone. If anyone had remained they would have seen that the biggest yew appeared to be surrounded with a corona of light for a moment, which could have been due to the moonlight, and then that too faded.

The trees stood in silence over the months as the man's body returned to the soil, as they had stood many times before. It was the way of all living things; to live, to grow, to die, to return at last. Over the years many were returned to the Earth and much later, in their turn, Druce and later still Oriana's spirits were returned to the through the biggest tree, as Gildas' had been before them.

The group of seven yew trees grew tall and magnificent, and they stood for tens of centuries, close grouped in their circle, sentinels of the land. The needle-shaped leaves that covered the trees in natural spirals of glossy green, terminated in blunt points. Every summer the tree was dotted with bright, scarlet berries. As the trees aged, the branches, which had formed a boxy shape, matured into classic cones. Finally the circle of trees reached their maximum height of seventy-five feet and upward growth stopped. By then, as with all old yews, they had multiple trunks and were hollow.

The people had worshipped and venerated them as they silently communed across the years, through occupations, and invaders' attempts to tame the wild land and its people. Powdered leaves from the trees were sometimes used to medicate any members of the tribe who had appeared to be possessed by an evil spirit. The powder would stop them writhing on the ground, and make their trembling limbs be still. Care had to be taken though, because the whole tree was very poisonous if used badly. The seeds were ground and used to make poison arrowheads, which were very effective at bringing down even large animals. Fallen branches were used to make the spears and bows and the arrows themselves, because of their great strength and flexibility.

The sacred circle of yew trees were silent witnesses to the rising and falling of the sun and moon, and the passing of the seasons. They saw birth and life and death and birth, amid snow and sun and wind and rain. The groups of people that came to communicate with them changed over the years as they died, and were replaced with young blood. The young bloods in turn became old and withered, and fresh young things took their place. The trees seemed eternal, compared to the meagre lifespan of man.

For a long time, the communal spirit of the Earth, and guardian of all living things, was pleased that its first children, the trees, which were forever connected to it by their roots, were held as sacred.

Things changed over the centuries. Gradually less people came to visit the Sacred Yew Circle, as man became seduced by power. As he gained this transitory, material thing, he gradually lost sight of the precious and eternal connection he once had with the Earth beneath his feet. Man strove for convenience above all else, and grew to prize possessions above knowledge. The old Gods were condensed down to just one, as religions became big businesses that competed for members. Which particular one God or Goddess this should be, was the question that started many wars. Religions fragmented and new dogma and belief systems spelt the end of the circle of sacred yew trees. New sins were created and defined that consisted of worshipping the 'wrong' God. People were dragged, some unwillingly, into a new 'dawn'. A dawn created not by Gods, but by man.

In 1406, on a bright and blustery October day, just after dawn, a group of men approached the circle of yews, which by now were gnarled and twisted, ancient and creaking, but still strong. The men carried axes, scythes and shovels that flashed in the sun. The men were noisy, chattering and laughing among themselves, and they disturbed the energy around the trees. The yews comprehended that danger was approaching, and yet they could neither flee nor protect themselves. All they could do was to send out a message of distress to other trees in the area. Had the invasion been of insects or disease the trees would have been able to make themselves unpalatable, or develop immunity against them, but against man, who saw himself made in God's image, they had no defence. The animals, birds, reptiles and insects could flee, and they did, running, flying, slithering and scurrying, desperately seeking new homes in the trees and grass that grew further out from the circle. Some of the men tried to catch and kill the beasts that fled, and soon bloody corpses lay around the circle.

The men carried flagons of beer and bundles of bread and cheese. Some of them wore crosses around their necks and these occasionally glittered just like the blades and tools, just like weapons, as the daylight caught them. After a short discussion, most of the men set to with a will, slashing and chopping at the circle of trees, and if the trees screamed, then it seemed that nobody heard them. The men appeared to give no thought at all to the carnage they were committing, and were not aware of any spiritual connection to the trees, which they felled with axes.

One by one the majestic trees toppled, crashing to the ground. As they hit the hard earth they shattered, branches splintering off and hollow centres revealed. Chunks of timber flew through the air hitting the other trees that still stood. Then the fallen were stripped of their branches, and finally chopped into small pieces. As the day wound on the men took breaks to swill the ale and eat the bread and cheese, surrounded by the brutality of ripped and torn limbs and the crushed and drying, needle-like leaves, some dampened for a while by the blood of the slain animals. The air was filled with a mixture of the aroma of resin, and that of fresh meat.

The men were obviously well-instructed and well-motivated, and by late afternoon, every living plant, every blade of grass, every seedling, and every scrap of life, was torn from the fifty-foot circle that had once been held as sacred. Then the trees' roots were scraped and pulled and dug from the ground, leaving it dry and dusty, while the digging dragged up stones and rocks from underground to lay on the surface. The men lit fires, sending swathes of thick white smoke up into the air, as the wet remains of their destruction were burnt. The sacred grove once known as *Seven Sisters,* and a place of worship, was now a no-man's land on the far outskirts of a city known as London.

Gone were the lofty natural cathedrals of yew, with their vaulted, spiky ceilings of interlaced branches, patch-worked with jagged blue swatches of sky. Gone was the soft moss that had sprung underfoot when revellers had danced. Gone was the deep carpet of needles, softened with age. Gone were the white daisies that had been braided and worn around wild red hair. No more would the hallowed whisper of the wind be a prayer to Gaia. Nothing new took root or seeded in this ground. It was as if it had been blighted, its energy drained. The surface was dusty and gritty and covered with a mat of stones, from tiny pebbles to rocks. Ash was littered everywhere, sometimes in heaps and sometimes sprinkled like dirty snow flakes. The smoky entrails from the smouldering trees writhed skywards, like the wisps of dying souls.

Paganism had been outlawed, and all the sacred groves, like the yews, were cut and burned, except for those few that survived on sites chosen to be the homes of the stone churches of the new religion. New churches would spring up among the trees. The creator was now to be worshipped in other places, in man-made, stone magnificence, even if they would never rival nature's own temples. From now the one God would be prayed to and worshipped in sterile stone edifices that lacked the soul and spirit of His own minarets, and nature's creatures would be forgotten, and the fact that they were the very best of God's creations would be buried, and only remembered underground.

# Chapter One

It was a chilly afternoon on 16 October 1687. On the rural outskirts of London the breeze sighed and mourned over a big empty circle of stony, barren ground. What had once been a grove of sacred yew trees, full of vibrancy, was devoid of life, and had been for centuries. The fifty-foot circle had once had plumes of stately foxgloves in the centre, where the acid needle-leaves of the yew hadn't fallen, but it now stretched empty and dry. The grass that had grown around the foxgloves was gone too, as were the white daisy-heads that had peeped shyly from it. The wind made an eerie whistling noise as it raced among the dry rocks on the ground, compressing itself through holes, ravines, and cracks in the stones.

A crow flew overhead, a faint, shadowy silhouette in the failing light. The infant metropolis of London had sprawled in the opposite direction, and the wind was blowing the wrong way to carry any sound from it in the crow's direction. All that it could hear was the seeking, keening wind. The faded shadow of the crow sped over the circle like a wayward ghost, rippling over the rocks.

In its mouth the bird was carrying an acorn. It had collected the oak fruit from the nearby forest that grew across the track from the once sacred grove. As it flew over the empty, blighted land of the circle, it seemed as if perhaps the crow's dim thoughts might have been turned to its roost and safety and to get there before nightfall, because it suddenly lost interest in its burden. It cocked its head as if something down below had spoken a command, and its beak opened as if involuntarily, allowing the acorn to plummet to the ground. The acorn bounced and rolled and came to rest against a jagged rock, which jutted from the ground like a stalagmite, at the edge of the old circle nearest to the track. The crow glanced down briefly, as if in wonder at what had made it drop its bounty, but, loathe to touch down on the blighted soil, it flew on, homewards.

The acorn lay there, dormant. It could sense very little. Cold. Dry. Nothing quivered inside it, and no life strove to emerge. There was no point; the soil would never support it. Normally, even an acorn in fertile soil would have only a one in ten thousand chance of becoming a tree, and this acorn's chances were apparently, virtually non-existent. Yet it waited all through the long winter, quiet, patient, and content to be where it should be.

\* \* \*

One night, in the early spring of 1688 a scruffy-looking man drove a pony and rickety trap off the track and right onto the lonely spot, where the acorn still waited. The small, roan-coloured pony was fretful, snorting as it was forcibly steered onto the barren ground. It halted obediently, but the man had to engage the brake tightly, and wind the reins around the handle, before the pony would stop pacing on the spot and trying to drag the cart away.

It was a cold night, and the stars pierced the ever-darkening sky sharply, as if they were impatient to fire darts of frost onto the Earth below. The lonely hooting of a tawny owl, and the eerie scream of a screech owl, floated on the crystal air and wafted across from the forest, the sound bright and clear. The man would have preferred to have hidden his deed in the depths of the forest on the other side of the track, but he needed bare ground to dig a grave in, and the forest floor and its undergrowth were too thick to allow it. Anyway there were too many wild animals and Lord knew what else roaming the forest at night. Animals brought hunters and poachers out after dark, and he wanted no witnesses. Despite the coming frost, a bone-freezing north wind was blowing, sending dust fountains scurrying around the man and the pony, stinging their eyes and numbing their faces.

The man didn't like this empty spot any more than his pony did. It was cursed and haunted. But at least no hunters were likely to ride across it later and perhaps discover what had transpired there this night, and uncover what was soon to lie beneath the cold ground. The man shuddered, pulling his filthy cloak tighter around himself as his breath clouded in front of him. He was ragged and dirty and had a look about him that would have made any decent person turn the other way if there had there been anyone to see him. The area was deserted as he had expected it would be. No-one else would be foolish enough to visit this place in the dark and cold.

He had once been a young man who had been full of optimism and hope for the future like many others, but the struggle to survive in the back streets of London had forced him to turn first to petty theft, and then to greater crime. There was no way that a poor man could live under the law. Without crime to fill his pockets, he would have starved on the streets. Finally, his soul had reached a place where lawlessness was natural, and crime was just a way of life. This wouldn't be the first time he'd killed for money. There were always those that would pay someone who was willing, and desperate, rather than getting their own hands dirty. This wouldn't be the first time he'd helped the smugglers dispose of a witness or a double-crosser.

With a quick and furtive glance around, the man got down from the trap. He took a moment or two to steady the pony, patting its neck and putting his hand on the bridle, to make sure it wasn't going to try and drag the cart away. Satisfied, he went to the back of the cart and started to drag off a shape that was shrouded in sacking. The bundle was obviously heavy, and the man grunted with effort as he manhandled it off the trap. The thud of hitting the hard ground brought a sharp cry from the bundle. It squirmed and started to make muffled, squealing noises. The noises and the strange movement startled the pony, and it snorted and pranced sideways in fear, threatening to snap the brake and take off, leaving its owner stranded. The man thumped the wriggling bundle randomly to quieten it, and hurriedly dragged it a few yards away from the frightened animal, which calmed enough to stop fighting the brake, but still had the same air of anxiety as its master.

The man dropped the bundle again, with a, "Be still, or it'll go worse for you!"

He took a knife from his belt and slit open the sacking. Inside there was a young girl, aged about fifteen years. She was bound head and foot and gagged. Moonlight whitened her face, and its light made her start squealing again, as she took in her surroundings. The pony snuffed and snorted again behind them, and the man cuffed the girl about the head with his knife hand, "Quiet, damn you!"

She was dressed in fine looking nightclothes that were nowhere near thick enough to keep her warm, outdoors on this freezing night, and her feet were bare and clotted with the mauve of cold. Blond hair straggled around her head and her bright blue eyes shone with terror. Her eyes grew ever wider with fear as she took in the knife, and her squealing subsided to a panicky moan. She closed her eyes for a moment, trying to shut reality out, but her fear made them open again. She was horribly desperate to see what was happening, though she dreaded it. She was too tightly bound and too dispirited to try and escape, so she stayed still on the rough ground, tears welling silently and pleadingly from her eyes.

"You saw what you shouldn't," the man mumbled by crude explanation of her fate, "Smugglers don't take kindly to snooping eyes!"

The girl was called Primrose Lawrence, and she was the daughter of a Doctor and his wife. She had lived with her parents near the Port of London, near the 'Devil's Tavern', a well-known smugglers' haunt. Just outside her bedroom window there was a flat roof, and she used to sneak out there to watch the night sky. The previous night she had been perched on this lofty and seemingly invincible platform, and had watched some rough looking men dragging a hand-barrow, heavily laden with bulky sacks, up the slope from the dockside. Little had she known that the barrow was laden with tea and French brandy. She'd had no way of knowing that the smugglers would be hanged if she had reported them, and so were willing to quickly resort to violence against anyone who might bear witness against them.

Half-way up the slope the barrow had tipped and a sack of tea had fallen to the ground. The men had sworn with raised voices as they were forced to stop and pick it up, hanging frantically onto the barrow at the same time, to avoid tipping off their more fragile and more precious cargo of bottles of brandy. Primrose had giggled in her innocence as their crude words and oaths had floated up to her where she sat, never dreaming that her girlish voice would condemn her to a terrifying destiny.

The smugglers had heard her laughter, and stood back, alarmed, looking up to see where the noise had come from. They had spotted her spying on them, and even though she never understood what she had seen, it had been her death warrant.

The next night the ragged man had been sent to snatch her from her bedroom, and by the time she had been brought to the clearing, her parents had still not discovered her absence. The last thing she could remember was being snatched from sleep by terror as she'd realised that someone was looming over her bed, then a sharp pain in her head, and then sudden and deep darkness. She didn't know what was to happen to her now in this desolate place, but her heart knew it was going to be something evil. For her there was no hope, and for her parents there stretched ahead only the despair of a lifetime of never knowing what had happened to their child.

Primrose was in shock, as she lay bound and gagged on the cold, cold ground, shaking and waiting for her end to come. The chilliness and dampness of the earth permeated her clothes and made her muscles go frigid and numb. Her mind whirled, searching for some sense in the situation, but failing. She felt her reality start to slide, and thought that this was what brought visions to her terrified mind. She could see an old man lying on the ground near to her. She could see through him, and she knew he was not of her world. An equally ghostly antlered headdress was on the ground in front of him. He rested against a tree trunk that was also transparent and non-existent in Primrose's world.

Despite the fact that she was tied hand and foot, Primrose felt herself floating upwards until she was looking down on the old man, as he took his last breath of life. A hand that could have been her hand, save that her own, real hand was bound, reached out and rested on the old man's head as he gasped his last. Surely already a spirit, nevertheless he died without a sound and with just a smile of acceptance on his lips. His head slipped away from her fingers as he slumped further over, falling against the phantom tree trunk. Primrose felt grief and happiness both as the old man's body gradually faded till it was barely visible, and then seemed to vanish into the tree's trunk. She was less afraid of the spectre of the dead man, than of the very real assassin who held her fate in his hands.

Mercifully, her mind had been dimmed somewhat by the vision, and she was not so aware of her surroundings, so her fear faded into the background. She was apart from her body in some way. Somewhere in the recesses of her mind she saw herself walking with a group of people, walking away from the old man's body. She could hear faint chanting all around her, and for some strange reason it comforted her, making her feel that everything was alright, and that despite her plight, she was not, and never had been, alone. She knew that whatever happened at this time, her time would come again as it had before. She could feel the frigid earth beneath her leather-clad feet, and the crackling of icy twigs as she walked on them. Whatever this strange world was, it seemed more real to her at that moment than her present one.

The ragged man leapt back into her consciousness, his knife outstretched. Showing a modicum of mercy with the speed of his attack, he leapt upon Primrose, and quickly slit her throat. She felt almost no pain, just a warm rush travelling down her body, and as her sight dimmed and grew dark, Primrose could still see the group of her people walking away. She felt light grow around her, wrapping her in comfort, and she willingly melted into it, at peace.

As the girl's blood soaked into the sacking underneath her, the murderer quickly wrapped her back up in her rough swaddling, muttering charms under his breath, to ward off her spirit so that it couldn't possess him. He stood up, panting, partly from fear of what he had done, and partly from the exertion. Taking a spade from the trap, the man started to dig. The acorn was dislodged in the first shovelful of earth, and it lay in the slowly growing pile of soil. The ground was as unyielding as it was sterile, and moments later the man was sweating and cursing.

"Damn ground! Hard as nails!" he complained, his fear now totally driven out by anger and exertion. For him, it was back to normality, and he thought little more of the girl whose short life he had just destroyed. His only thoughts were of escape from blame for his crime, and the ale and food he would buy with his payment from the smugglers. He wasn't even a really evil man, his reality was one he had to live in and struggle with daily, and one is which 'survival' was the only watchword.

He frantically scraped and stabbed at the frozen ground, sure he was about to be discovered. A few more minutes later, and he was ready to give up. The hole was just long enough and wide enough to take the bundle, if he pushed her knees, which had not yet stiffened, into a bent position, and doubled her over.

Once he'd laid the body in there in a tight foetal curl, and covered it, it would only be a few inches below the surface. He shrugged. No-one would see it after all, out there, away from hunting land or habitation, and in a haunted spot. He shoved the soil back over the body, not noticing the acorn as it tumbled back into the hole and nestled on the sacking against the girl's heart. He tamped the ground down with the flat of the spade. He spent a few more minutes covering the mound with rocks and stones gathered from the barren circle, so that the wind wouldn't soon scour the gritty soil away and reveal the body.

Then the man made a ragged cross shape in the air three times over the grave. This was not a prayer to the new God that had taken over the country, or for the grace of the soul of his victim, but a token gesture to the old Gods and Goddesses of the Earth. It was an acknowledgement to the ancient sacredness of the place, a brief nod to the ghosts of the ancient sentinels that had once stood there. It was for his own protection, to ward off any spirit that might think to follow him home. With a last cursory look at the sad mound, he turned and got back in the cart. He released the brake at last and the pony, more than ready, surged forwards. Nevertheless he drove the pony on faster, unnecessarily severe with the whip, because suddenly he seemed to be in a hurry. The pony cantered off, dragging the cart behind it, and gradually the sound of its hooves faded into the distance, and silence, save for the howling wind, returned to the desolate grave site.

Under the ground the edges of the sacking were stained with the girl's blood. Underneath the body the fluid was sucked greedily into the parched and thirsty earth. The blood also enveloped the acorn where it lay, on the girl's chest, and its shell turned red. From death, as the cycle turned again, life was born. Something stirred inside the heart of the acorn as it sensed the fluid nourishment that it had been given, and a spark from Primrose's soul ignited its life-force with extra energy. Fibres inside the nut stretched and twisted, and the tiny, budding concept of a shoot was born inside the blank shell. Life called to the acorn's tiny spirit, as nature decreed that this time an oak tree, rather than a yew, should one day stand at the head of the old circle.

The oak was a symbol of balance to ancient people, its roots deep within the earth and its head in the clouds. Perhaps the soul of the

Earth could sense the coming battle that man would unknowingly fight, between industry and spirituality, and hoped that the oak would show him a way to unite both without destroying either. In the far off future the crossroads that would develop there would be called 'Dru Corner', instead of its official name, by people who would be totally unaware of its true meaning. This name came easily to the lips of people, who, though they would often separate themselves from the old ways, could not separate themselves from their own subconscious and ancestral memories so easily. (Dru – Oak).

The tree could not have burst into life and grown were it not for the girl's sacrifice, because the barren ground was so compacted by years of pounding wind and rain that there was little airspace and no oxygen for the roots to use. The girl's burial and her mortal remains broke up the soil and provided a place for the acorn to sprout, as well as nourishment. Without the acorn the girl would not have been able to leave a whisper of herself on Earth. It was a strange, mutual symbiosis of quite different consciousnesses. And yet on a deep energetic level both were intrinsically the same.

# Chapter Two

A few short weeks passed by, and the mere idea of a shoot became a real shoot. Drawn by the promise of light above and sustenance below, the acorn strove for life. Its spirit soared when the white, pointed tendril of its first shoot pierced a miniscule hole in the top of its shell, and then the shell split open for it to pass. At the other end of the acorn, hair-like filaments of root sprouted, and embedded themselves into the enriched soil underneath it. The fine tap root, the future tree's main artery, pierced the girl's body and drove deep into the soil beneath, anchoring the acorn tightly. The dead girl's spirit allowed a shadow of itself to be drawn into the acorn and the two entities were bonded. As the tree thrived, so did the girl's memory.

A week later a shower of rain watered the shoot, and it sprang into brighter life, surging upwards, as it turned a gentle shade of pale green. The acorn rejoiced as the sun's weak rays warmed its upward reaching shoot, and its tap root, growing thicker by the day, sucked goodness up into the centre of the fruit. Within another week, two fledging leaves had sprouted from the stem, which had turned browner and exchanged its delicate pale skin for a slightly tougher coat. The roots grew at the same speed at the shoot, matching its broadening. The tree's tap root dominated its system, while the smaller lateral roots, varying in gauge from the thickness of a hair to that of fine wire, spread from it, holding the tree against any sideways strain. Still, the tiny tree was very vulnerable, and could at any time have been eaten or crushed by a passing deer, standing alone at the edge of the eerie, empty circle. Strangely, nothing ventured into the clearing, except occasional birds that flew high overhead, and even they shouted warning curses as they did so.

As the weeks turned into months, the little tree grew bolder, sporting a brighter plumage of green. It was a good year. The climate was stable, and high summer came with its hot sun that warmed the leaves, which glowed with health under its light. Water became the most vital thing in the tree's life. While the tree was not too tall it wasn't too difficult for the water from the depths of the roots to be drawn up, but as the tree grew taller, it would find it harder to bring the moisture up to its highest branches, until one day it would reach the limit it could attain, and all growth would cease.

Nothing disturbed the tree's growth that year and it was quickly stronger and well-rooted. Most fledgling trees had to battle in the shade of their bigger ancestors, struggling for air, minerals and moisture, but this tree stood alone and aloof. Primrose provided the tree with all the food it needed as it broke her body down into its chemical and mineral elements, and it thrived. The rest of the forest flourished at a slower pace on the other side of a worn track from the lone tree and its barren circle. The oak tree did not feel alone in its solitude, it felt free to breathe and bloom to its full potential.

Finally the heat of summer gave way to autumn, and the tree's few leaves grew brown and wrinkled. One by one they fell until the tree was a naked skeleton again. Gradually winter drew her misty cloak down from the north, and the tree's roots stopped passing nourishment up into the trunk, storing it instead, getting ready for a new growth spurt in the spring.

The spirit of the dead girl had risen with the tree, giving her a different kind of life. Her presence gave the tree a greater awareness of the world around it. Its consciousness started to expand as well as its physical size. The tree could sense things. Food. Moisture. Warmth. Light. Vibration. Cold. Dry. Danger. Disease. It could also sense the strongest pull of all, that of Earth consciousness. At all times the tree, and Primrose with it, felt at one with the energy that nourished their spirits, and knew that one day it would call them to return home.

The seasons passed, and no especially dry summers or long winters came along to stress the tree or inhibit its growth. By the spring of 1692, a strong oak sapling stood firmly rooted into the rich soil. It was five feet high and had sprouted its first few twig-like branches, and those branches had lobbed leaves. They shimmered in the sunlight as they were tousled by a gentle breeze. The little oak's bark was smooth and unlined, like a young baby's skin, and at six years old it was still a baby. Its infant roots now curled around delicate bones, but nobody knew of it.

The days ebbed and waned as the tree silently and slowly grew. Nights came and went and solitary owls flew overhead, like ghosts in their deathly, silent flight. To the tree the world was a calm and quiet place, filled with warm sunshine, soft rainfall and caressing winds. As the girl's memories rose in its sap, it had some awareness that the world could be a much colder and terrifying place than it knew, but for now the tree knew only stability.

A rough lane had been worn, fifty feet from the tree, and was one of the main routes into the City of London. The forest still grew on the other side of the road, dense and dark, making the lone tree appear even more alone, standing as it did at the edge of the barren ground, which had still spawned no other life. To the side of the tree away from the road the land was empty and flat, save for the stones and rocks, which had lain undisturbed for centuries. The bare circle, some fifty feet in diameter, was rarely crossed. Animals and humans alike shunned it, and many thought the spot to be haunted. People reported strange chanting coming from the area around the tree, and the occasional lone traveller had his blood frozen by an eerie scream renting the silence of the night.

The tree enjoyed its solitary existence, the girl's memories being its only company. The only thing that disturbed it was the occasional noise and vibration from an isolated carriage that passed over close enough to cause a quiver in the soil, softly brushing against the fringes of its root system.

A year later and the scene had changed. Man multiplied in an uncontrolled way, not patient as the acorn had been, not willing to wait until there was sustenance readily available for it. The City of London had grown bigger and the amount of people rushing to walk its streets had increased with it. Carriages passed along the road quite frequently now, and their vibration sometimes shook the tree's roots, but they were strongly embedded, despite the friable, dry soil around them. The tree sensed that some battle had begun.

The oak got its energy from the sun. The big bright star was the catalyst for the process of photosynthesis. Each of the tree's leaves took in sunlight and carbon dioxide, mixing them with water and food from its roots. This made a sugar-like food that fed the tree. It silently breathed in carbon dioxide through its leaves and exhaled oxygen, which helped keep the planet in balance, and keep the tree content.

One night the oak's eventual contours were to be shaped by man. There was a full moon casting her magical white light over the landscape, and she chased and harried the shadows that were cast by the rocks and stones at the roadside, as she dodged among the few clouds that fled across the sky. The tree's spindly branches waved in the moon's light like skeletal fingers reaching upwards, and its woody soul bathed in the silent path of the moon, taking a different energy from her.

The sounds of a carriage could be heard approaching. As it hove into view it was revealed as a big one, with four horses at its head. It was being driven along the dirt road at a fair speed, and the rattling and bouncing of its wheels was loud across the previously quiet scene. Four people, two men and two women, rode within. They had been at a ball in the city and were making their way homeward to their country estate. Sounds of talk and drunken laughter drifted on the night air.

With no warning a terrifying figure on horseback galloped from the forest edge, caught up with the carriage, and speedily overtook it. It was highway robber, the scourge of travellers and the romanticised figure of many a young maid's dreams. The coach swerved wildly as the driver tried to get past the outlaw. His name was Jack Durham, and he was the son of a nobleman. In his youth Jack had been idealistic and tried to help the poor with his family's money. He soon learned that altruism was considered weak and pointless, and that it was thought that the best naturally survived. He had turned to the romantic crime of robbing the rich to feed the poor. Little did he know that rich man or not, he would soon swing from the hangman's noose.

In his concealing mask, Jack turned his horse in front of the carriage, his pistol raised. "Stand and deliver!" the dreaded words rang out.

With horror at the sight of his worst nightmare coming true, the coach driver yanked harder on the lead horse's reins, flailing with his whip at the same time, steering away from the robber. The carriage swerved even further from the road, and one wheel passed over the oak sapling, crushing, and dividing its stem into two, just above a pair of fledgling branches. Sap bled from the wounds to the tree, trickling down like sticky tears. The tree screamed silently into the night at its loss, unheard and un-mourned.

The highwayman overtook the coach again, and pointed his pistol square between the coachman's eyes. The horses were soon dragged to a quick stop by the driver, and Jack jumped down from his horse, leaving the black mare blocking the coach-horses. They seemed nervous of her, snorting and pacing on the spot, and she stood and eyed them, her ears flat back, her nostrils quivering. Jack walked to the carriage door, pistol still cocked. The driver took his chance and now that he was out of the robber's gaze, he jumped from the other side of the carriage, and made off. He ran with the speed that only the threat of death to a coward can produce. The highwayman ignored the driver's craven departure. He had his eye on plumper prey within the carriage. He stood six feet tall and broad of shoulder. His dark hair cascaded from beneath a cocked hat, and his eyes, covered by a mask with eye-slits, were dark and hard. The Highwayman had a full mouth, and he smiled triumphantly.

"Out!" he commanded. The door opened and four passengers shakily alighted into the moonlight. There were two young ladies and two older gentlemen.

"I'll s...see you h...hanged!" one of the men protested, stuttering, with his fat belly wobbling in fear as he shook. The other man seemed afraid to even speak.

Jack laughed. It was a threat he'd heard many times before, but he believed that no-one would ever come close to knowing his identity.

"Money! Jewellery!" he demanded.

The ladies cowered behind their men folk. Rumours had made them afraid for more than their riches. They squeaked and whimpered, holding their skirts tight about them. Hurriedly, the passengers all removed their rings and necklaces. The men handed over all of their jewellery, pocket watches and pouches of coins.

Satisfied at last that he had got all that was to be had, the highwayman whistled his coal black horse. The mare trotted to him obediently, and he swung up onto her broad back. Laughing again, a chilling sound to his victims, the bandit galloped off towards the forest.

The ladies sighed with relief that the robber hadn't molested them; the men blustered about how they would never rest till they killed him, and how the driver would be horsewhipped for deserting them. All of them would capitalise and dine out on their wildly exaggerated experiences for weeks to come, but they would never guess that the vicious highwayman was actually the son of their neighbour. In their stories, the men would become heroes who drove the villain off, and the women would have charmed the rogue with their beauty, till he was unable to steal from them.

After a few moments of self-congratulation the group started to look around uneasily. This spot had an atmosphere about it. Cutting short their chatter, and realizing that they were still vulnerable out in the depths of the night, and from more than ghosts and ghouls, they all climbed back into their carriage, except one of the male passengers, who ascended to the driver's seat to take the reins. He shook them up and the carriage moved off, gradually disappearing into the night, the sound of it gradually fading, until all that could be heard was the hooting of the lone owl. Thirty minutes later the driver emerged, sheepishly, from the forest. He looked around, sighed, and then set off for home.

The oak tree had been split by the carriage wheel, but it didn't die. The tap root had been twisted in its bed, but the tree's will to survive was very strong. Some slender lateral roots had been torn, but those that remained intact instinctively tightened their grip on the bones and soil beneath them. The sapling drew more energy from the matter in the earth beneath it, and instinctively concentrated it in the area of the split, to encourage healing. The tree grew and slowly it healed itself. As it grew on, the trunk became twisted and scarred, with a hump where the trunk had sealed, but the sustenance it took from the body that its roots entwined around kept it strong.

In 1698, in the spring, an old woman crept up to the oak tree under cover of darkness. Her name was Nerissa. She lived alone in a little shack deep in the forest. She was a crone, a wise-woman, often called upon to treat sick people and their animals. She was also the nearest thing the local people had to a midwife, and she provided vital services to them. And yet her position and her life were always in danger. She was looked upon with awe and fear in equal measures, because the people had been taught to suspect and dread one such as her, as being in league with the devil. Yet they often needed her help, and desperation would bring them to her, eager to make her acquaintance with coins, and then just as quickly renounce her as soon as they had what they wanted.

Nerissa had been brought up by her Mother and Grandmother, both 'wise women'. Both the women's husbands had left the family home, afraid or ashamed to be married to women who were looked upon with fear by too many people. Threatened by the possible outcomes, they had decided to go off and find new lives, and new women, together. Nerissa had never known her Father or her

Grandfather. From an early age it had been obvious that she would grow into her Mother's shoes. She had been taught well, both in her trade, and in her fear of being denounced one day. Now she lived alone, both her matriarchal ancestors having passed on when she was but twenty.

She whispered words of encouragement to the tree, telling it that the sacrifice it was about to make would be used for the ultimate good, that of healing. She placed both hands on the trunk of the tree, and could feel the vibration of its life-force as it surged upwards inside, taking water up to the highest leaves. This was more easily felt in the spring when the stored-up goodness that had been kept in the roots all winter was being released into the body of the tree, as it was now. She laid her head against the bark, and felt an energy exchange between her and the vibrancy of the tree. For a moment she felt she was one with the planet, and knew her rightful place in the universe. For a moment in her life she felt unafraid.

She felt bad about mutilating the beautiful oak, but folk would buy the medicine she made them for their fevers from the bark of the oak tree, so long as she never revealed the sacred words or rites she used to help convert it. She lived in constant fear of being labelled 'witch' for practising the craft that had been handed down for generations of her Mother's family. Death would surely follow such an accusation. And yet she knew that a life lived in denial of one's predestined purpose, was not lived at all, and so, despite her fear, she carried on with her calling.

She carried on too with her collecting, despite the sounds that caressed her ears, sounds that seemed to be coming from the tree. It was distant, whispered, chanting. Dreading that some evil spirit might suddenly pop from the tree if she gave the sounds any heed, she clapped her hands over her ears until the noise stopped. If there were some spirit trapped inside the tree, she didn't want it to latch onto her and follow her home.

Removing her hands slowly from over her ears, she tested the air. All was silent again. She moved around the tree, her sharp knife catching the moonlight and sliding it down the blade to the branches that she was slicing the bark from. If the tree could have flinched from her knife it would have done. She was careful only to choose branches that were a good four inches in diameter, so that the tree wouldn't sicken from its loss. They also had to be smooth and blemish free to make the best medicine. From the bark she would make a decoction for reducing fevers, diarrhoea, dysentery, tonsillitis, and laryngitis. After she had enough bark, she went on to collect leaves to crush for the treatment of wounds, cuts, burns, and inflamed eyes. Later in the year she would return to collect acorns to make into an invigorating drink.

She muttered to herself as she worked, asking the tree's forgiveness for her theft, and a man who was making his way home down the road, heard her mutterings. Not seeing her there cloaked in the darkness as she was, he hurriedly crossed himself as he came within earshot. Because he couldn't see the old woman, he thought there was no-one there but invisible spirits. He could just hear whispers and detect odd movements and shadowy shapes. He held his breath, and didn't exhale until he was past the spot. He considered the area to be haunted and evil. He had to walk this stretch of road every night on his way home from the Manor, and many a time as he'd passed the same tree and felt sure he'd seen goblins or ghosts lurking in its shadows. Now as the weaving shapes danced and cavorted, he was sure the tree and the ground around it were polluted with evil. He hurried onwards, almost running, until he was well out of sight of the tree.

Nerissa carefully put all the bark she had cut into a pocket in her rough cloak. Before she made her departure she bobbed and turned several times, thanking the tree for allowing her to take its bark, even though it had been given no choice in the matter. Then with a last furtive look around she scuttled off into the darkness, returning to her dank and lonely wooden cabin.

The tree bled sap into the bare patches left by the removal of the bark, and girded its loins to heal itself once more. The sap grew sticky and dark and protected the delicate inner flesh. Slowly the patches grew knobbly with blobs of thickened sap until the armour plating was strong enough. The fragment of the girl's essence within the tree recognized the strangeness of humans, who would burn one of their own for trying to heal them, and as always, the tree shared her knowledge.

# Chapter Three

On the night of 26th September 1703, the largest of a series of violent storms swept across the countryside. The wind at times that night exceeded a hundred and twenty miles per hour. The tree was lucky. It was sheltered by the forest on the other side of the track. A great swathe of trees was felled within the forest as the roaring, screaming wind tore through the night. Trees whose roots had been weakened by the previous high winds, toppled easily in the face of the biggest storm they had ever known. The wind hurtled high over the lone oak like a demented banshee, but the tree remained untouched, just swaying like the mast and rigging of a tall ship, adrift on a tossing sea.

By the summer of 1725, a forty foot high oak tree, with a gnarled and twisted trunk stood on the patch of ground next to the road. Its bark had changed from its once youthful smooth silvery texture and had become rough and deeply fissured, sprinkled here and there with grey and yellow lichen. Mid-way up the trunk was a bulbous, thickened waist where the two stems that had once been severed had fused back together. It had stout branches that flared outwards forming a wide canopy, and had become a landmark at the new crossroads that bisected the land. Some called it the hanging tree because of its location at the crossroads, though no-one had yet swung from its branches.

The ground around the tree gradually became more attractive to birds and animals. The tree was wiser as well as older. This May had seen the first catkins on its branches; tiny insignificant male flowers and even smaller and less significant female flowers. Later in the year, jays and magpies alighted in the tree to feast on the first acorns it had ever produced. The birds pulled and tugged at the pointed fruit, prising them out of their little pixie-cap cups. Any that were dropped by the greedy birds were snapped up by deer and wild boar that passed beneath. Squirrels came to collect the booty too, preparing for winter, biting out the hearts of the acorns, so that they could be stored without sprouting. Thousands of insects, weevils, butterflies and moths moved in and lived within the crevices of the tree's craggy trunk. Woodpeckers and pigeons lived among its branches, and forest animals, such as hedgehogs, feasted on its fruit. The tree became an oasis of nourishment.

People came and went, flourished and fell, prospered and failed, fought and loved; racing through their lives, mostly in the frantic pursuit of material gain. It often took them longer than their own lifetimes to understand where real happiness could be found. The tree simply grew. It drew in the air and water and minerals it needed to sustain it, and no more. The tree understood that it had all it needed and was content. The fragment of Primrose learned and passed knowledge that could be understood by it, onto the tree.

In 1764 there was great activity in the forest the other side of the road from the lone oak tree. Men armed with saws and blades arrived by carriage and cart and on foot. They made their way into the forest and marked out thousands of trees with chalk. Then they started to fell oak trees in large numbers. The air was filled with the noises and men and horses and the sounds of chains as they were thrown around the felled trunks. The chains clanged and rattled as the downed trees were dragged away by horses. The men sometimes sang, sometimes shouted and sometimes cursed as they worked. To those who might hear, the trees were also filling the forest with screaming.

Men do not have the capacity to hear or sense the communication waves that plants send out in response to an attack. If they did, then on that day the forest would have resounded with the sounds of trees in distress, echoed in ever increasing circles throughout the acres of woodland as the message was passed on. The lone oak tree responded with 'waves' of its own, reacting to the carnage it could feel, and reacting to the danger it could sense.

During the second week of work, two men walked across the road towards the lone oak tree and stared at it, appraisingly.

"It's big enough," said one, through his pipe.

"Aye," replied the other, "but that twist….will make it difficult. The Navy only wants straight planks for their ships."

"We'll see if we reach our quota, over there," – he pointed across at the forest, "Maybe come back for this one later. We'll be able to salvage some straight timber from it."

They walked back to their workmates to continue the unheard and un-sensed carnage.

Luckily for the lone oak, the men cut enough trees from the forest to fill their need. They left swathes of bare land, punctuated by the stumps of thousands of trees, like fields of jagged graveyard markers. It took months of pillaging and burning. All this was to make vessels to take the sailors and soldiers across the ocean, in order to kill other men, whose names they would never know, by the thousand. Most of the men who fought and died would not have much idea what they were actually fighting about, theirs just to do or die. The entire fleet of twenty-seven ships that were built for the war took 50,000 oak trees in all to build, representing two million years of tree growth.

By 1775, wild flowers had taken seed around the tree. The seeds had been dropped there from the shaggy coats of animals the tree had encouraged to come to the clearing. They had been left there in bird dropping as those creatures perched in the tree's branches. It was as if the one tree had gradually restored the land it stood on. Over the seasons its leaves had enriched the soil as they were dragged below ground by earthworms, making it receptive to the seeds. Cowslips and rosebay willow herb, toadflax, fragrant agrimony, betony and cow parsley all embroidered the soil of the once barren circle. As the flowers bloomed, people no longer shunned the ground, as its sterility was replaced by colour and life. The area became popular with folk, and people often picnicked at the base of the tree. The tree itself welcomed its new small flowering neighbours, because they didn't steal too much water from it, and they brought more insects and animals to the tree, which it needed to help fertilise its own seeds.

At this time the tree started to detect strange new chemicals in the air. Little did it know that it was already feeling the effects of man's continual striving for convenience at the expense of the planet. Far away factories were springing up to make glass, clocks and china. The Industrial age had begun. Chemicals were being spewed into the air by chimneys taller than trees. It was not enough pollution to seriously damage the tree, but every little scar and nodule it developed from that year would be like a tiny time capsule, storing the chemicals it absorbed, until the tree became a living history book of man's mistreatment of the planet's air.

On a balmy summer evening in 1775, a beautiful girl of eighteen arrived at the tree with her sweetheart. As it was past 10pm, dusk hid the couple from view, and they were also concealed from anyone passing by the now broad trunk of the oak tree. Above them the oak leaves rustled softly in the dark, and the brushed shadows painted the ground with dark, weaving shapes. The scent of wild borage, heartsease and forget-me-nots perfumed the twilight. The girl had raven black hair and dancing eyes. She was at once a picture of innocence, and a siren, drawing the boy in. She was as irresistible as she was forbidden. The secrecy and the feeling of being alone in the world added spice to the tryst for both of them.

The boy was nineteen years old, tall and dark and dangerous looking. His eagerness flattered the girl, and she felt like the centre of his Universe. She had never felt so beautiful or so desired. He seemed like some mysterious wild animal, drawn to her by his male instinct. The feeling was overwhelming to her. He took her into his arms, and she shivered with emotion.

The girl and the boy kissed and caressed, until the girl started to draw back, protesting, "No more, we must not."

The boy whispered words of love to her. "Do you not love me, as I love you?

"I do, of course I do, but my parents…"

"We will be wed."

Still she hesitated, "Maybe when you return from the fighting."

"A soldier may never return from battle, you know that. Before I go to perhaps die in a far away field, let me hold you. Let me have a memory that I can die with. Let me have a memory of your sweet body to carry in my heart and make me brave while I die for you."

His romantic turn of phrase was just what her young heart was waiting for. She could resist no more and sank to the ground beneath the tree, opening her soul to her lover. The night was filled with the sounds of love-making. The girl had been a virgin, and she cried out briefly as he united with her. The boy had been experienced, but the night, the wildness, and the forbidden nature of his conquest meant he moaned in the strongest ecstasy he had ever felt. Because of this his words of love were true, for the moment at least.

The leaves of the tree sighed in the breeze, like the stealthy breaths of a secret watcher, while the lovers rested, wrapped in the comfort of each other's arms. Finally, murmuring endearments, they rose from their makeshift bed of flowers. The boy took out a knife and began to carve into the tree bark. The girl stayed on the ground looking up at her lover. As the knife flashed in the starlight, she suddenly felt afraid, as if the blade was about to be plunged into her defenceless body. She gasped as she sensed suddenly that her arms and legs were tied. She held her hands up to her eyes and looked at them in awe, because she could still feel them bound at her back. She gagged at the feel of a rough cloth over her mouth, and rubbed a hand across her lips. She whimpered as she saw the gleam of a dagger as it plunged towards her throat. The young man she had just lain with took on the appearance of an old, dirty man as he reached down to her. She gasped at the vision.

The boy was bending down to see what had alarmed her, and as her eyes met his, the spell was broken.

"Are you alright?" he asked.

She smiled languorously, "Yes, my love." She dismissed the dream from her mind deciding it was just the effects of the heady passion between them.

He smiled in return, and went back to his task. He carved their initials within a heart on the tree trunk, cutting deep into the bark, so that beads of sap rose to the surface, like colourless blood. His told the girl that his mark would be there forever as a testament to their love, but in the depths of her mind she could still feel herself being covered with soil, and she shuddered and then cast the feeling away.

The tree suffered the wounds of their initials being carved, and the cuts were not of much consequence to it, now that it was so much bulkier.

The couple met many times at the tree, making it their regular trysting place. Each time the boy talked the girl into giving herself to him with promises of a future and words of loving flattery.

Four months later, the girl met her sweetheart beneath the tree for what was to be the last time. It was the beginning of October and the tree's leaves were turning yellow and brown. Soon they would be falling. The earth around its base was littered with acorns, and a squirrel that had been disturbed from collecting the booty, and had fled up the tree to safety, chattered angrily from above. A chill current of air trickled around the branches and had lowered the temperature to that of near winter. The atmosphere was full of fear, and the boy felt uneasy as he waited.

When she arrived at the tree the girl was sobbing. The boy took her into his arms, asking her what was wrong, promising her that he would defend and protect her no matter what had befallen her. She told him that she was pregnant.

The boy's loving nature was immediately eclipsed by anger and recrimination, and his previous persuasive warmth turned as chilly as the air.

"No! You fool!" he protested, and then asked, callously calculating, "How do I know the child is mine? How many others have your lain with?

She clutched at him, terrified and hurt, "You know I love only you!"

But he pushed her away and took no notice of her pleading. "So you say, but women are fickle creatures, and you cannot prove that the child is mine, can you?"

"No," she cried, "But I swear..."

He ran from her, without another word, mounted his horse and rode away at speed, leaving the girl to cry her for broken heart. She leaned against the tree trunk, sobbing, her fingers finding the carving in the bark, and tracing it with her fingertips over and over again.

Two days later the tree bore witness as the same young man who had broken the girl's heart, rode his horse down the road at a gallop. He was being closely pursued by another older man on another horse. The older man was waving a pistol in the air as he bore down on his quarry. The young man swerved desperately and headed for the shelter of the tree, where he had lain with his young lady only days previously. He passed behind the broad trunk in the nick of time as a report rang out, and the bark of the tree was sprayed with pellets. The young man escaped into the forest, but the tree bore the scars for evermore, the pellets embedded deeply in its flesh.

Late the following April, a carriage pulled up beside the tree. The girl alighted, carrying a baby in her arms. She took the baby to the tree and stood under its branches. The leaves were still small and new, a very bright acid green. The spring sun shone through the lacework of branches, highlighting the leaves and spraying delicate swaying patterns on the ground beneath it. The girl walked around the trunk until she found the carving the boy had cut. She held the baby girl's tiny hand in her own and placed the finger-tips on the carving. She had called the little girl Jasmine.

"This is all you have of your Father, Jasmine," she told the child, "He was a soldier and he was brave and strong. He died for us. He loved you, but he had to leave to go to war. He loved your Mamma more than life, but he was forced away from her." Her lies came easily, because she had come to believe them herself. "As you grow, you must come here every year and touch this place, in memory of him."

She gestured to the coach, and the man who had been riding up next to the driver got down, an axe in his hand. He stopped beneath the tree and looked to his mistress. The girl nodded and the man stepped up the lowest branch of the oak tree and swung his axe. The blade bit through the bark and into the greenish white flesh beneath. The whole tree quivered with the force of the blows as its limb was severed. Jasmine started to cry, as if she sensed the pain of the tree. Her Mother soothed her. With a crack the branch gave way and tore itself from the tree, hitting the ground hard with its weightiness. The tearing left jagged points and shards of the branch sticking out. The man lifted one end of the hefty branch.

"Is it enough?" the girl asked him.

"Yes, M'am. This will make a fine cradle," he answered.

The girl believed what her Mother and her Mother's Mother had told her; that a baby who slept in a cradle made of fresh oak timber would grow strong enough to defeat anything, even goblins. The girl had been betrayed by a man, not a goblin, but still the idea comforted her. She never wanted her daughter to be used and abused as she had been, by anyone, human or not.

She turned to leave, and then hesitated as she caught the distant sound of singing, or chanting, but it faded quickly, and she thought it to be a trick of the wind. Her mind had grown closed to such things. The driver got down and he and the other man dragged the severed branch over to and onto the back of the coach. Then the girl and her party got back in and drove away, leaving the damaged tree to frantically send out warning pulses, telling other trees in the area that there was a predator around. For a long time the tree was in severe danger from micro-organisms that would have brought disease through the broken stump, but the wound slowly dried out and gradually the shock to the tree's system passed, and the tree lived on.

That winter a strange procession made its way past the tree. It consisted of hoop topped wooden wagons pulled by hairy, docile horses. The vehicles were brightly painted with flowers and stripes and signs of the zodiac. Loose foals ran along beside, occasionally stopping to grab a mouthful of grass before trotting quickly to catch up with their dam and the cart she towed. Dogs travelled under, inside and alongside the wagons. They reached the circle next to the tree and started to pull off the road, forming a circle that matched the circle of ground. Once they were all stopped, the horses were un-harnessed and allowed to roam freely among the flowers. The people seemed as if they must be resting in their wagons, as all became still and quiet. The dogs slunk underneath the wagons and curled up to sleep.

Until recent years the Roma had travelled from town to town with their extended families in plain carts, but a few years previously they had adopted the brightly painted bow-topped tent-wagons with canvas roofs. Some of the wagons were ornately carved, and one or two of the wealthier families had wagons trimmed with gold leaf. The wagons always drew admiring glances from the villagers as they passed through, and many a young lass was lured from her family home by the dark handsomeness of the Roma lads and the promise of a romantic, nomad life. The wagons held all the essentials to live, a cosy bed and a stove, but the people lived most of their lives outdoors. A lot of people called the Rom, gypsies, erroneously believing their dark skins meant they came from Egypt. They actually came from India originally, and they had become an essential part of the structure of the country, providing a movable band of casual workers. The Rom worked during the spring, summer and autumn, setting up camp on the edge of the towns, but in winter they liked to find a permanent site away from the towns, to rest up in. This particular family had spent the year hop-picking and bean gathering in Kent, and had come back across the river for the winter.

As darkness fell the people emerged from their mobile homes, and a large fire was built in the centre of the circle. The Roma gathered around the campfire, and cooking pots that were soon wafting aromatic steam up to the stars, were placed on top of the burning wood. The children settled in front of the fire at the feet of the 'storyteller', and the tales of old Romany ways were told to their wide eyes. The storyteller spoke in English but also in Romani. The meal was prepared and then eaten around the fire. Once this was done, the songs began, and the night air around the oak tree was once again filled with the sounds of music as it had been in the past.

A young boy called Hezekiah, wandered away from the fire. He felt secure in the darkness, because he could still hear the voices of his family behind him. He was drawn to the big oak tree. He'd noticed it as soon as they had stopped in the clearing, and had been eagerly awaiting his chance to talk to the tree. As he neared its massive trunk he could feel the energy emanating from it. He smiled at the feeling and reached out, placing both hands on the knobbly bark. Then he went in closer until his arms were around the tree as far as they could go, and his cheek was pressed up against the corky, flaky wood.

He nodded, his hair rasping against the bark as it moved up and down.

"Yes," he whispered, "Yes, I see. I do see, but, it is not the time. Stay there sweet child, where you are safe and warm, and wait with patience until that part of you that is not balanced becomes balanced again. Life and death are both fraught with uncertainty, and until you are certain of your path, do not move. Time will turn and your time will come, but not yet." He made a stroking movement with his hand against the trunk, smiling again. "I will visit you again."

He moved away, and walked back toward the firelight, and the dancing flickers lit up his dark, curly hair from behind, making a golden edged halo of it. By the time he was seated at the fire again, the dancing was about to start and this was Hezekiah's favourite part of the evening's festivities. His sister, Nadia, had emerged from her wagon, her scarlet, fringed skirt swirling as she walked. Her improvised dances were legendary among the family. It was very late before the family all went to bed that night.

Each night for the duration of their stay, the Rom filled the circle with music, bringing energy back to it. The family stayed by the tree for two months, and by then the grass was muddy and churned. The horses had eaten it and both they and the dogs had soiled on it, the feet of both and those of the people, mixing the manure into the earth. It was good for the land. Over the coldest months the frost did its job too, breaking up the soil. As it warmed towards the spring the ground was enriched with bacteria and moisture retaining mulch. The next year the circle was brighter and greener than ever and the flower seeds that had been spread in the tramping, blossomed ever further.

# Chapter Four

By late October 1805 the tree was broad and tall. It had been a long, hot and dry summer and so its autumn leaves were coloured and wrinkling. A few fell in showers with every gust of wind, skittering along the ground with a rattling noise like swarms of beetles. Winter would come early this year. The small, round, brown orbs that were the homes of the oak gall wasp larva bulged incongruously and alien on some of the branches that had already been stripped of their leaves. Light green orbs of mistletoe sprouted from its higher branches.

The mistletoe would soon be covered in white berries, and the globes that sprouted on the trees in the forest would be harvested by eager children anxious to earn a few farthings. They would sell it to those celebrating Christmas. It would also be gathered by superstitious village folk who believed it would keep evil from entering their doors if they hung it above them.

One cold day two men rode towards each other along the London road. They met and greeted each other beneath the tree, reining in their horses to pause on their journey. The horses' breath blew streamers of white vapour into the chilled air as they snorted the blood-warmed air from their lungs. The two men were rosy-cheeked with the cold. They greeted each other, and then their topic of conversation turned to the death of Lord Nelson and the fall of Napoleon Bonaparte at Trafalgar.

They had thought, they said, that Napoleon was going to finally invade England, and were glad he had been thwarted, even though it cost Admiral Nelson his life. One of the men patted the trunk of the big oak tree they sat beneath, and commented that it was lucky to have escaped being felled and turned into timber for ships. They blamed Napoleon's arrogance for his defeat, saying that his captains had found it impossible to obey him.

They discussed that despite the fact that Napoleon had amassed two thousand ships and ninety thousand men along the coast of France, he had still been no match for the British blockade. One of the men commented that Napoleon's last and ultimately fatal mistake had been to order his fleet to sail out and meet the English enemy ships, which sat quietly waiting on the green Atlantic swells at Cape Trafalgar, eighty kilometres from Cadiz. Admiral Villeneuve had set out with a Franco-Spanish fleet of thirty-three, with two thousand, six hundred and forty guns, to engage the enemy. Although this was a massive force, their destruction was inevitable. Napoleon's pride had been his downfall and had over-ridden all his previous strategic genius.

Villeneuve had been, the men said, haunted by the memory of his humiliating defeat by the much smaller English fleet only three months earlier, and even Napoleon had begun rightly to mistrust him. Yet despite this mistrust Napoleon had foolishly laid this onerous task on him. Added to this was the fact that the Spanish ships were mostly manned by soldiers or beggars who'd been press-ganged, and therefore had been less than loyal to their masters, whereas Nelson's ships were crewed by men who adored him and were willing to die for him.

The two men laughed at the stupidity of the French General. To think that he could beat the most skilful captain of all time, Horatio Viscount Nelson! With the Admiral's death, England had lost its saviour, but still it *was* saved. England was inviolable! The two men bade each other farewell, and rode away in opposite directions.

By this time the forest on the other side of the road had started to thicken again after its harvesting, and younger oak trees once more stood among the other deciduous trees. The animals that needed the oak trees had returned too, and the air was filled with the sounds of birds and insects as they went about their daily business.

One night in the autumn of 1810, a violent thunder storm crashed through the high branches of the lone oak tree. Thor crashed his drums overhead, and spat his lightening forcefully into the dark sky. Jagged arrows of light flashed down to the earth. Cloudbanks raced across the landscape, and were artfully and dramatically lit by the bright moon that slipped occasionally between them. The limned edges of the cloudbanks contrasted with the plumy centres, which looked even darker by comparison. The wind had been strong all night, but as dawn broke it seemed to gain extra strength from the coming promise of daylight, and become even more determined to damage the oak tree.

The tree writhed in the wind, which partly strained it but also made it joyful in its dance of freedom, even while it was being damaged by it. Its branches and still green leaves tossed like a crazy, giant mermaid's hair, or as if the dead girl within its roots was rising once more to life from the depths. Her essence danced in the wind with the leaves, and its breathy voice as it blew through the branches could have been her voice, raised in an eerie song.

If it had been weeks later and the leaves had already been gone, the tree wouldn't have fared so badly, but because it was still fully laden with leaves, the wind used them to gain a purchase to twist its branches, and small twigs clattered through the branches and bounced onto the ground. Still the wind was not satisfied, and it twisted among the foliage even more. Suddenly there was a loud crack as one quite big upper branch gave way to the pressure. It creaked as it split away, and hung by a thread, barely clinging to its life-giving connection to the tree. The wind squealed in triumph and shrieked even louder.

Finally, with the full dawn the storm abated and the thunder faded to a distant rolling again. It rumbled on, reverberating around the valleys for a while, and then quite suddenly there was complete silence. For a few seconds it reigned, and then birdsong started, gaining momentum with the growing birth of the day, as pink sunlight peeked out from behind the scudding clouds. Under the tree it still seemed to rain as its leaves shivered in the now, gentle breeze and loosed the water that had collected on them, sending it down in showers. The torn branch creaked as it swung. For the tree this injury wasn't as bad as the others that had been inflicted on it, for this one had been done by the wind, its sometime natural ally, and could therefore be forgiven. In the quiet, the broken branch let go of the tree and tumbled downwards, lodging against a low branch, rocking gently with every breath of air.

Later that day the wind had died down completely and the weather had calmed into blue skies and sunshine. Footsteps were gradually evident as someone tramped along the road. A young, bearded man came into sight and walked along the lane towards the tree. He was whistling and was obviously a bright and happy person. As he came closer to the tree it became equally obvious that he was a very preoccupied young man. His unfocused eyes showed that he was thinking, thinking, always thinking, but not about this time or this place. He lived most of the time in some other world, peopled with dreams and imagination.

When he reached the crossroads, instead of turning one way or

another at the junction and following the tracks, the young man
walked straight on across the sward, leaving the road without even
realizing he'd done so. He crossed the dirt and grass unseeingly, and
almost walked right into the tree trunk before he noticed its bulk in
his path.

"Ah," he said, to no-one in particular, sticking out a hand as if to
ward the tree off. He stared at the bark, walking around the tree, and
then peered closer, reading the initials carved there years previously,
by the young lovers. He traced the letters with his finger. He
examined the speckled buckshot that peppered the bark on one side.

"Um...," he muttered, pursing his lips, totally engrossed in his
observations. He looked up and noticed the dangling branch.

"Poor old tree," he commented. He reached up and tugged at the
branch. Without too much effort it came free from its last connection
to the tree and tumbled into his waiting hands. It was heavy, and
slipped from his grasp, tumbling to the ground. With effort, the
young man picked the branch up and cradled it in his arms. It was
quite short but chunky with a big feathering of leaves at the end. He
sat down, balancing the branch across his lap, humming gently to
himself, and resting his back against the broad tree trunk. He spent a
few minutes gazing into space and then he got out his whittling knife
and began to chop off the leaved section, stabbing and gouging until
it was free. Then he began to carve the main branch.

His connection to the tree through its trunk and severed branch
seemed to take the young man off into some other realm. He worked
diligently, mindlessly, it seemed, hacking away big pieces, and then
becoming more delicate in his movements, sculpting smaller and
smaller features into the white wood. It was very difficult as the
wood was fresh and sappy, splitting rather than cutting cleanly, but

the knife was sharp and his will was obviously strong. Now and again he cursed softly as a splinter tore off in the wrong place, but mostly he hummed and whistled to himself.

Several hours later, the sun was sinking fast and the young man apparently realised how long he'd been sitting there under the tree.

"Oh dear," he muttered, glancing at his pocket watch, "Aunt Agatha will be wondering where I am." He patted the tree absent-mindedly and got up. The carving he'd worked so painstakingly on, rolled to the ground, but by now the young man's attention had wandered to some other place, and he left it there, forgotten. He hurried off, stuffing his watch back in his pocket and muttering about being late.

A week later two small boys came down the road. They were scruffy, aged about 10 and dressed in clothes that didn't quite fit them. One boy had split and gaping shoes; the other had none at all. They were talking animatedly as they walked, and gesticulating in the air in the way of small boys in their imaginary world of play. They had a stick each and wielded them at each other like swords.

Charlie and Georgie lived in the nearest village. They had been given a big list of chores to do, but had managed to sneak away to play instead. Now they were hungry and weighing up the advantages to going home for food, against the disadvantages of being unable to escape their chores for the rest of the day.

As he lunged with his stick sword, Georgie said, "I'm hungry and I want…" Stab. "…to go home!"

"It's alright for you!" Charlie stabbed back with equal energy, "You don't have to go back to well-digging!"

Swinging his stick over his head, Georgie responded, "Cleaning out the hogs ain't much fun y'know!"

Suddenly Georgie broke off his attack as he noticed a shape under the tree, and he stopped playing and pointed, "'Ere, Charlie, wot's that?" he asked.

The two boys both hurried across. They were very excited to find a wooden toy under the tree, even though they had no idea what it was. It was a blocky shape with a narrow funnel carved carefully onto the top. It had wheels, but no shafts and no horses to pull it. It was taller and narrower than a carriage, and the wheels were fixed and joined to each other by rails of some kind.

"It's a carriage, Georgie," said Charlie, picking it up.

"Don't be dumb! It's got no 'orses and no shafts or nothin' and those wheels can't even turn!" said Georgie.

"Lookit this – somebody's wrote their name on it!" Charlie announced, tilting the toy so that his friend could see them. "Can you read it?"

On the side, some initials had been artfully carved. *GS*, but neither boy could read. Georgie did recognize the 'G' though, as being to do with his own name.

"Don't know 'im," he said, stabbing at the 'S' and taking hold of the toy, "But 'it's got my letter on it, so 'is loss is my gain!"

Charlie tightened his grip on the toy, and they started pulling it back and forth between each other.

They paused. Georgie had hold of the narrow funnel, and both boys recognized that they were dangerously close to snapping the toy.

"Ere," said Charlie, "we could maybe get money for this..." He looked his friend meaningfully in the eye and slowly let go of the toy.

"Yes, you're right. We could buy some cheese and ale and we

wouldn't need to go home to eat, and then we wouldn't have to do chores!" agreed Georgie.

The two boys hurried on, still squabbling over who should play with the toy first before they took it to the market to sell.

The sounds of their arguing faded into the distance, and the wind sighed through the oak tree's branches as a part of it disappeared forever. Once more the tree's survival instinct fought off disease from its damage, and it could have been that perhaps the fragment of Primrose was what helped it to live on.

# Chapter Five

One dark night in 1834 a strange light appeared in the sky, high over the tree. A tiny, glassy, milky ball, swung through the darkness overhead, chased by a vaporous tail that seemed to propel it, surging it onwards through the sky. The tree stood silently in the darkness, whirling through the infinity of space on its own, green and blue ball, as the comet passed overhead. The ways and wonders of the universe were all accepted pragmatically by the soul of the tree, for its spirit understood its mighty place within the energy of the cosmos. The girl's small essence wondered if it should try and break free and return to the stars to reunite with the rest of her soul, but she could not. Her home within the tree seemed to have become permanent, and though she was now ready to move on, she found she could not escape.

The next day, a group of men going to their work trudged along the road by the oak tree. Their words caught in the breeze and were fragmented by it.

"Mark my words…"

"No good…end of everything…"

"Master says we should have no fear…"

"The rich will be saved…you can wager on it"

"Aye, tis us will sicken and die…"

The next night the comet passed by again, bringing more terror to the simple folk who only saw it as an omen of death and destruction. Their lives were so transitory that they lived in fear of its end the whole of their time. They rushed towards their deaths like travellers in a hurry, never pausing to see the magic that surrounded them. They never saw the immensity of the universe, or of their own spirits. The tiny part of the girl's essence however, trapped as it was within the tree, started to get a glimpse of all she really was, and with that realization came hope.

By the summer of 1837, thick grass had grown around the tree, giving the flowers a soft green bed to peep from. Half-buried acorns from the mother-tree had begun to find enough sustenance to germinate, from the rotted leaves that had been shed over countless autumns, enriching the soil, but they never thrived. Each one was eventually grazed away or carried off half-open by a squirrel, badger or hedgehog. The trunk of the tree itself sported a beautiful bright green coat of moss on one side, so thick that it resembled the verdant, hairy coat of some alien beast. Because it had no peers nearby, the moss was only on its north side, whereas on the trees in the forest, the moss grew all around the trunks. The oak, like some giant craggy king, in its regal green cloak, wasn't ready to accept competition in the shape of fledgling trees. The lone oak tree now measured one hundred and forty feet in height and it towered over the scrubby land and the seedling trees of beech and birch that tried to sprout here and there in the grass, waiting for a chance to take over. But it seemed that the land itself wasn't ready to support other trees either, because they all withered in their first year.

One warm afternoon a carriage drew up several hundred yards from the oak tree, and a family alighted. The Mother, Jasmine, the Father, Gerrard, and their three daughters, started unloading a picnic hamper from the carriage, helped by their two coachmen. Strangely, the eldest girl of the three, Josie, was also the smallest, with fragile bones, and delicate features, and she headed straight towards to oak tree, running as fast as she could, despite her family calling to her. Reaching the tree, she threw her arms as far as she could around its massive trunk, her soft cheek nestling against the green mossy coat.

The child's parents smiled indulgently. Jasmine might have preferred another spot, as the tree and the ground around it had unhappy memories for her. Jasmine was the daughter that had resulted from the union of the young lovers under the oak tree. She had gone there for years to revisit and touch the initials carved into the tree by her Father, believing him to have been torn from her, his child, by war. She had always noticed that her Mother's bitterness seemed worse when she was near the tree, but had assumed it reminded her of her grief for the brave, dead soldier.

However, Jasmine had eventually discovered the truth about her birth and how her Father had abandoned them. The initials he had once carved now made her sad and angry. Although the area was one that her family loved to come to, she herself always tried to stay away from the oak tree itself. But if darling Josie wanted to sit under that particular tree, then the whole family would agree. Josie was 'simple', but she made up for that with her sweet nature and her affinity for all wild things. Her health was delicate and everyone treated her with tenderness. The man, Gerrard, was not her real Father, but he treated her with the same love he gave the other two girls who were his real daughters. The family carried the picnic trappings to the tree, spread out a blanket and started unpacking the feast.

Josie still hugged the tree as if it were a pet bear. She could feel the energy pounding up through the bark, like a giant heartbeat, where a less sensitive soul would sense nothing. She was gradually *drawn into* the tree, and became one with it. Then she could sense the other trees across the road and see their energy rising like fireflies ever upwards. She felt her own soul soar with them. She could hear distant whispers that sounded like singing, streaming past her ear as it pressed against the green woolly moss. She heard the swish of a knife as it parted flesh, and the crying of a child. In her mind's eye she could see a child, its chubby fingers pressed to some initials that had been carved in the bark of the tree, and she knew that the child she sensed was her Mother, Jasmine. Her fingers searched for and found the carved initials. Josie's eyes pricked with tears at the sorrow she felt for the little girl who had been her Mother, and had known no Daddy. The singing turned to chanting in her head, and she whirled away from the tree, following the sounds, dancing delightedly, skipping after the group of people she could see walking towards the brow of the hill. "Oriana!" she called out.

Her parents laughed at the sight of their pretty little daughter capering gracefully to music they could not hear. They would never experience the world that she saw and felt, and never realised that *they* were the losers and she was the wealthy one. To them Josie was an unfortunate soul who didn't live in the real world, and they put it down to the unfortunate circumstances of her birth.

Jasmine's Mother had given birth to her, out of wedlock just like her Mother before her, and for a while it had looked as if her life of shame and her early death were footsteps that Jasmine would follow. Little Josie had been apparently born to suffer physically and mentally for her Mother and Grandmother's shame. Jasmine however had gone on to marry Gerrard, despite having a bastard daughter, and she had been relieved and joyful that the other two girls she had born within the confines of wedlock had been unscathed by the disgrace. Josie's Mother, Father and sisters, being normal, thought they were the lucky ones, never realizing that they were unable to connect to the magic that walked in step beside them, for their whole lives.

"Mamma!" Josie cried, "The singing people are here again! And Oriana is here! *You* are here!"

"Yes, darling, but come now and eat."

Josie waved at the people she could see wending their way from the tree and disappearing down the slope. The link snapped. She sighed deeply at the loss, but then ran across to join her family. The tree and Primrose also felt the severing of their link with Josie and the past, and their inner cores quivered.

Josie's sisters were excitedly discussing what they would wear to the upcoming coronation. The next eldest sister was fourteen years old and wanted a new bonnet to replace her hat at the very least, to keep up with the changing fashions. The youngest, at thirteen, had her eye on a pair of new boots, preferably fastened with a row of tiny buttons. Jasmine, their Mother, was hoping for an entire new outfit, and dreamed of boasting the new hourglass silhouette, with a tiny corseted waist, pulled in by laces and a strong maidservant. They all three smiled at Josie, amused by the fact that their dear sister and daughter never thought about anything of the important matters in life. The amazing royal event would go quite unnoticed by Josie, who would only gasp and smile at the horses and carriages and vivid colours of the clothes and flags.

While the two coachmen stood guard, the family passed the afternoon. Jasmine and Gerrard sat quietly in the shade and read. The two younger girls had brought a toy theatre, which they set up, ready for their audience. Josie wandered among the flowers, stopping every now and then to speak to unseen creatures in her gentle voice. Sometimes a butterfly would alight on her hand and she would coo to it delightedly. Occasionally she would cast wishful glances towards the slope, her eyes bright as she strained to catch a morsel of the singing that might drift across the centuries.

In late 1838 the crossroads were deserted. Silence hung in the air as if waiting expectantly for something. There was no birdsong, and no rustling in the undergrowth. All the beasts and the air itself were still. Then the pregnant peace was broken by a strange sound. A distant, regular beat could be heard. As the sound grew closer and closer, with infinite slowness, over days, the ground started to vibrate. It didn't trouble the tree, whose roots were strong and deep, but several birds flew from its branches in panic, and a hare scurried away from the flowers it had been poised to eat.

After several days the sound reached its peak. It was distinguishable now, and seemed to be the steady hammering of metal on metal. There were also the sounds of many men and wagons. The men were talking, laughing, and singing at night around campfires that glowed in the distance. The sounds came to their closest, although still not close enough for the source to be seen, and then just as gradually, over several more days, the noises faded again, back to eventual silence. The birds and animals settled down, and the tree's roots settled again.

Weeks later another noise, somewhat similar, but different too, could be heard in the distance. This time the source approached much quicker than before. The noise grew louder yet and the tone became more distinct. There was a chuffing, puffing noise, followed by the sound of men shouting and the squeals of high pressure steam. The noise came closer and closer. Yet even at its closest the cause of the sound still could not be seen, but over the hill wisps, and then clouds, of white steam could be seen, billowing up into the cloudless sky likes hot dragon's breath.

The cacophony got louder and louder as it passed at its closest point, and the vibration became almost like an earthquake as the ground trembled. Birds and animals fled from the strange thunder and the whole tree actually quivered to its roots. A piercing whistle rent the air into shreds, and then the noise and the steam slowly receded until silence and stillness returned at last. It took several hours for the air, and the energy, to return to normal.

Over the next few months the thunderous sound was heard at regular intervals, until at last most of the wildlife ignored it. The only disturbance it caused was when the birds called out in alarm to each other, as they would have done had there been an earthquake or volcanic eruption coming.

# Chapter Six

In 1856 a rag-tag bunch of wounded soldiers rested in the shade beneath the oak tree. They were marching home from London, having been recruited from the out-lying villages and towns, months and years previously. Now they were headed home again, to the towns and villages they had been torn from, to lives once whole, now in shreds and tatters. They had visited mysterious foreign lands that once they would have dreamed of, but had seen only mud, bloodshed, and death there. They were travelling in small groups, some being pushed along in wooden barrows by their fellows. They were for the most part, young men, but they looked old and broken. Many had missing limbs, with bloody stumps where strong young arms and legs had once been, bandaged heads, and other horrendous injuries. Some of the men talked in low voices, and some of them were silent. Worse were the ones who just moaned.

There was not one completely sound man among them. The walking and the slightly wounded were glad to be alive, and yet despairing of what kind of life they would now lead, and what use or burden they would be to their hard-pressed families. They knew that times were hard at home, that everyone needed to be able to earn their keep, and they wondered what they had really been fighting for, and what their missing limbs had bought. They were skinny and undernourished and spoke with nostalgia and some expectation of enjoying once more the food their Mothers used to cook.

Most of them were exhausted and just lay on the grass, quietly resting. Two struck up a conversation about a nurse who had helped them at the hospital in Scutari. They talked of how she had taken the men from the filthy floors and given them clean beds.

"More of us were dying from the dirt than from our wounds, till she came along."

"It's true. I wish she had come sooner and then the cholera might not have taken my young brother, Albert."

Another man joined in the conversation, "I was at the hospital in Balaclava, and we had our own angel there, thank God. Her name was Mary Seacole. She was a black woman. A black angel."

The other two men glanced at each other, even their experiences of war and death not quite knocking out the streak of racialism that had been burnt into them since birth.

Noticing their expressions, the man continued, "Aye, I know what you're thinking and I might have thought it myself once. But see this?" He held up his left leg for them to see. There was nothing but a 9 inch stump. "If it wasn't for that 'black angel' I would have died where I fell. It fair gave me a shock when she fetched up next to me amid the flying bullets. Stopped the blood she did, and then half carried me from the field, never ducking from the shot, as if she knew she wouldn't get hit."

The other two men looked stunned and one said, "Maybe there be good in all races."

The other replied, "Maybe even in the race we have just finished trying to kill?"

The tree silently shaded them while they rested, and soon in groups of threes and fours, on foot and on crutches and barrows, the men went on their way, the fitter ones supporting or wheeling along their badly maimed companions.

All through the day and night, small groups of soldiers marched, limped and hobbled along the way. It was a pitiful parade that passed the oak tree that day and in the days that followed. The oak tree stood as silent witness to the terrible wounds that surely some dreadful unknown beasts must have inflicted on the men. Once they had all passed by, all that was left to mark their going were a few blood-stains in the soil and the odd scrap of bandage. It was terrible that so many whole young men had been reduced to dirty smears on the pages of the history books. Such is war.

In the high summer of 1888 two women walked by the tree. They were dressed in bright silk and lace. Finery it seemed, and yet there was a dusty, slight raggedness to their appearance. They wore gaudy necklaces, too bright to be anything but cheap paste and beads, the metal tarnished and dull. The colours of their clothes were a little too vivid, a little too obvious, and just a little bit too dirty for them to be mistaken for 'ladies'. Their conversation could be clearly heard in the still of the day.

"Sliced from ear to ear, and her entrails ripped out..."

"My God Millie, I think we got out just in time to save us from the madman! Why do you think he wants to kill us working girls?"

"There's no way to read the mind of a maniac, Rosie. Maybe he got turned down by his lady love and he takes his revenge on us poor souls. Maybe he has no lead in his wick and blames women for it."

They drew level with the oak tree, and decided to sit and rest for a while.

"Rosie, where are we going to go? What's to become of us?"

"We'll be alright. There's men everywhere who need the likes of us."

The two women brushed at their clothes ineffectually, trying to knock the dust from them.

"We shouldn't have run in such a hurry. I only have the clothes on my back and a few coins," said Millie. "I fair panicked after seeing that hacked about body. Didn't take time to pack anything."

"I have two dresses in this sack," Rosie held it up. "We'll have to find customers right away as soon as we reach a town else we'll not eat tonight." She paused. "I'm scared of more than the 'ripper'. I've heard tell that the women-folk outside of London, don't take kindly to our sort. I'm not sure we've done right. We could end up tarred and feathered, or worse."

"You didn't see the body last night. It fair turned my stomach. If you'd seen that you wouldn't fear other women."

"I know, but all the same. What's worse, the devil you know, or…?"

Millie followed the direction of Rosie's pointing hand as she gestured around, and stared at the forest all around them. It seemed to stretch for miles.

"What's that?" asked Rosie.

"What?"

"That...there! There's someone singing!"

"I don't hear anything," Millie insisted.

Rosie walked over to the tree. "I could have sworn…it was coming from here." She put her ear to the tree and listened. "Oooh," she said, "that made me feel all weird. Creepy, but I can't hear anything now."

"Dirty things, trees," said Millie.

Rosie stood upright, brushing minute particles of brown bark from her shoulder where it had been pressed against the tree, "Yes, I hate the countryside," she complained.

"I suppose…if we went back…the chances of us being his next victim…"

"If we stick together…"

"Never go out alone…"

"Let's go back to the city. At least we know who our friends are there, and there's not so much…muck." She paused as the sound of a vixen barking ran through the air like a banshee scream. She shuddered. "Too many animals and stuff here too."

Her friend nodded her agreement and straightening their clothes with a more purposeful air than before, and the two women set off back the way they'd come.

"Nasty place the countryside. All that fresh air. Fair clogs up the lungs!" Rosie yelled. Their laughter drifted back to the tree.

# Chapter Seven

The oak tree was well into its prime in the year of 1896. It was two hundred and nine years old and one hundred and forty feet high. It had a mighty girth that would have taken several men to encircle it. It was a king among the undergrowth of brambles and fern that had now sprouted around it, and the mulch from its fallen leaves over the years had prevented anything growing too close to be able to steal water or nutrients from it. One day it could have a forest around it too. By now the tree had a massive canopy, which provided dappled shade for any animal that sought it. The canopy was also home to many butterflies, in particular the Purple Hairstreak, which never strayed far from its food source all its life. Aphids spread their honey onto the leaves of the oak, and that was ambrosia to the butterflies. In the warm summer evenings they could be seen spiralling from branch to branch, like bright splashes of paint amid the dark green.

The tree's mighty arboreal world contained a complete miniature ecosystem for all its inhabitants. The night air and rain provided water that collected conveniently in its leaves and crevices. Ants scurried up and down the trunk and branches, providing food for larger insects like beetles, and nurturing their aphid herds, which in turn fed the butterflies with honey. Birds fed in turn on the beetles, and spiders trapped unwary flies of all kinds. Other caterpillars apart from those of the Purple Hairstreak ate leaves and wove intricate cocoons that would one day burst open to reveal another gorgeously hued butterfly or a dowdy moth. Bugs of all kinds burrowed and tunnelled with the tree's body, and never left its confines for their whole lives.

It was time for the oak to propagate in the ground around it that had become more fertile with the many annual carpets of leaves that had been shed. The leaves had been dragged below and turned, by the magic of nature, into rich soil. The animals that grazed around the tree had dropped dung onto the ground, which over the seasons had been broken down by frost and added to the mulch. The oak was ready to share its domain with others. It sensed that its life was not endless and that now was the time.

The spring started an important year. The tree had produced its best crop of acorns the previous autumn, and six of them had started to break into life. They had been buried by a squirrel, but that was only a small part of the miracle that took place. Something, perhaps the spirit of Oriana, had decreed that the time had come for a new sacred circle to form. Squirrels normally bite the 'heart' from the acorn before they bury it, to stop it from sprouting, but this squirrel, as if instructed, had buried them whole and undamaged.

When the squirrel had 'planted' the acorns, no-one save the spirit of Primrose was there to witness the amazing event. It was a red one and it had come from the forest. Its jaunty tail had flashed across the treetops as it approached. As if drawn by a signal it had crossed the track, looking full of purpose, its tufted ears twitching. Its bright black eyes had darted this way and that as it had neared its goal, perhaps puzzled as to what was pulling it to an area that was strange to it. It had scampered up the oak tree and spent some minutes apparently carefully choosing a fruit. Then grasping it within its hand-like front paws, it had examined the chosen acorn. Seemingly satisfied the squirrel had then transferred the acorn to its mouth and had run down the tree.

At the base, it had stopped, with its face a picture of concentration. It had twitched its nose and cocked its head, as if listening to something or someone. The squirrel had then started moving quite slowly, southerly, away from the oak, but neatly following the edge of the old sacred circle. It had stopped, looked around, and then buried the acorn, pushing it into the yielding soil with its clawed paw. Five more times the squirrel had repeated its actions, climbing the tree, choosing an acorn, and then burying it along the circle's edge.

Maybe by the power of Oriana's spirit or perhaps that of the tree itself, or simply by a synchronistic rightness, one by one, the six acorns had been buried in a perfect circle, with the big oak completing a ring of seven. After the passing of centuries, a sacred circle was once more forming, with the big oak at its head.

As the saplings grew and the circle clearly formed, it started to attract the attention of Pagan groups, and people who wanted to stay connected to nature. The circle of trees was unusual, because of the way the seven oaks had grown so symmetrically. No other tree spoiled the shape, either in the line of the circle, or within it. The Pagan group would perform their secret ceremonies within this circle. It worked especially well for them, it being a circle of seven, because they acknowledged seven directions within in. North, south, east, west, up, down, and centre being the seventh. One of the Pagans was a medium, and she started to pick up the dim presence of a young murdered girl whenever she walked near the big oak tree. Sensing that the medium was a channel that she might use, Primrose stove to find a way to talk to the woman, so that she might help the soul fragment break free. Unfortunately, though the medium was tuned into the universe, her tuning was not fine enough to pick up more that a tiny occasional spark from the girl.

The group venerated the oak circle and once again, apart from the noise of carriages passing by, everything was as it should be as far as the tree was concerned. In the Celtic Ogham alphabet, the oak is called Duir. This word is a mixture of Gaelic and Sanskrit, and means door. These people believed that the word referred to the oak being a doorway to inner strength and spirituality. They believed the oak was also a doorway into the spirit world, and that it would bring visions and a new understanding. A group of seven trees was especially propitious, because the Oak was also known as the 'seventh tree', central to the thirteen moons, and was therefore linked to the Summer Solstice. The Celtic year is divided into two halves, with the second half beginning in July after a feast in the Oak King's honour.

The Pagans believed that the oak tree was central to their growth and linked them closely to the etheric web, or communal soul of the Earth. Members of the group got 'married' there, 'jumping the broomstick' together. A year later they would often do the reverse and become 'unmarried' again. Babies were brought to the tree to be blessed and young children educated in the ways of the wild. For several years all was peace in the grove.

One warm and sunny morning one late July, summer was gently caressing everything in soft warmth. The air seemed not just to allow the butterflies to fly, but seemed to support them, so that they floated rather than flew. A raven landed next to the tree and gave itself a dust bath in one of the now few bare patches of ground. All was peace and serenity. The tree was home to many birds, and a woodpecker had enlarged and made a home of a hollow that had been formed the previous year by fungi. The young of the woodpecker's second brood were ready to fly the nest, fledged and feathered. A delicate, young fallow deer grazed in the grove, nibbling acorns and sweet young grass. Her chestnut coat gleamed in the sunlight, and her white spots dazzled.

Suddenly there was a distant bang, raucous enough to send the raven and the woodpecker into scared flight. The deer took to her heels and went springing across the road and disappeared into the forest beyond, with just a flash of her white tail to signal her departure. The baby woodpeckers fled back into the hollow as another noise took over. The trees themselves could not flee, but only stand and await their fate. It was a strange sound, a bantering, regular noise, like nothing heard in the wood before. It lacked the tonal quality of the steam train that by then ran in regular earshot. This was a new sound and as it drew closer, every animal in the vicinity scurried away and hid. No eyes witnessed the monster as it finally hove into view.

When the noise finally materialised, it was coming from a carriage, but a carriage with no horses to pull it. It rolled along on four wheels as if by magic, save for the noise, which was more demonic. Two men sat in seats up high, in triumphant control over the dragon, for dragon it appeared to be, with hot smoke pouring from its rear. The creature's smoke smelled badly. It also had big bulbous eyes on the front of its face that stared fixedly ahead, as would a predator's. Moving at hardly more than a walking pace, the machine trundled along the dirt road, and as they passed the tree, one of the men chose to squeeze a rubber globe, which emitted an ear-splitting hoot. Then the ground vibrated and the tree felt the motor's passing with every fibre of its root system, some of which now passed under the road. The roots quivered, but they were strong. The smell of the smoke lingered long after the beast had gone, poisoning the air.

Days later another motor car roared along the road, and days later, another. Before many months cars were not an uncommon sight along the road, and once one met a carriage and horses going the other way. At the sight of the huffing metal monster, the horses reared up and then bolted away in terror, dragging the carriage away from the road, and away from the beast. The man in the car, scarf flying in the wind, imagined himself a hero, and laughed at the coachman's predicament, as he struggled with the reins. The carriage passed beneath the tree and the coachman, too busy battling the terrified horses, failed to duck, so that the lowest branch hit him on the head, tossing him from the carriage.

He was not badly hurt, though bruised and shaken, and he jumped to his feet angrily, shouting at the car driver, as he roared away, albeit slowly, in his tin box. The horses, as horses do, soon outran their fear and stopped, snorting at the departing monster, but the coachman had a long walk to catch them. As he walked away from the tree he was muttering to himself about new-fangled machines, and how he was lucky his master and mistress hadn't been on board the coach, or that their precious horses hadn't fled all the way back to London.

The driver finally reached the horses and spoke to them gently to calm them.

"There my boys, never you mind that darned monstrosity. They'll never take your place, never you fear. Flash in the pan! That's all they are! No damn motor car will ever be able to travel these roads at speed, as you do. None will ever be able to daintily pick their way through rocks and mud like you do. The slightest puddle or bump and they will stop their noise, mark my words!"

Over the next few years, traffic of both the four-footed and motorised kind multiplied along the road, until eventually gangs of men appeared to break and crush rocks into the ground, making a firmer surface. After a few weeks the surface of the near the tree was finished and the men gradually disappeared further up the road. Peace reigned once more, apart from the traffic that passed by more and more often. It became a common sight to see two motorcars poised at the crossroads, each one daring the other to cross first, the drivers tooting their horns at each other in mock battle. Less often two cars would charge along side by side at their top speeds, and woe-betide any poor soul coming the other way, for he would surely have ended up in the ditch.

# Chapter Eight

A lot of even worse noises started to disturb the peacefulness of the grove in 1914. Loud bangs and whining sounds could be heard, especially at night. On 6th August 1915 a strange thing appeared in the night sky high above the oak tree. It seemed to float on the air and yet had no wings. It was globe-shaped and so big that it blotted out the moon, and hung there silhouetted for a while. Then the bangs and whizzes started, and projectiles whined overhead, streaking through the warm air. One hit the drifting object and instantaneously the sky was lit up by the fire and noise of an explosion.

There were several more small explosions, and every animal for miles around was startled out of its sleep. Barn owls and bats fled the sky in terror as flames seemed to fill the heavens. Then just as suddenly it was over. Burning fragments drifted down, fluttering among the leaves of the oak like powdery snowflakes. But these flakes were hot and smouldering. Some of the higher leaves were singed by them, and one large piece of burning fabric almost caught the tree on fire. It draped itself over a branch high up, and the leaves sparked briefly underneath it. Luckily, there was enough moisture in them to cool the heat, and the next day the cloth was dislodged by the wind.

Over the next few years the lane beside the tree was used by more and more of the motorised vehicles, and the smaller ones were joined by massive, smoke breathing monsters that occasionally rumbled by, shaking the ground with their weight and fury.

One day in the summer of 1940 the air was filled with the sounds of machines in flight. Day after day they would fight in the sky, firing at each other and many of them exploded or came crashing down in flames. As the years moved forward, bigger machines appeared and often dropped objects off in the distance that caused terrible noises when they hit the ground. One dropped into the re-grown forest opposite the oak grove, and trees were torn asunder, flying up into the air in chunks and showering down onto the other trees.

Men were doing what they did best again; killing each other.

Finally, peace descended again over the land, but it was not so for the tree. In 1955 men started felling the forest on the other side of the road. It took weeks and weeks of woody slaughter to clear the land. During those weeks hundreds of animals, thousands of birds, and millions of insects found themselves homeless. They ran, flew and scurried away from the destruction and gradually dispersed into the surrounding fields, hedgerows and woodland. The fragile ecology of the flora and fauna of the area was under severe threat, but no-one knew. Once again, Gaia, Mother of the Earth, eventually managed to absorb the damage.

But there was no saving the forest. The tree trunks were sorted, the best going to make solid oak, beech, and ash furniture. The pines went to make cheap cabinets and fence posts. The rest were sawn up, chopped up and pulped, going to make paper or to be burnt in domestic fireplaces. The ground was cleared and dug over with huge earth-moving machines that growled and vibrated, and then the trucks moved in. Lorry-loads of bricks and cement were unloaded onto the site, dust falling onto the oak tree, coating it with a powder like light snow fall. Foundations were laid, and a complex warren of some 500 quick-build houses took shape where once there had been only green.

Families that had overflowed the East End of London, moved into the houses, and birdsong and the soughing of the wind through leaves were replaced by the sound of children at play, radios, the occasional new-fangled TV, and lawn-mowers. The peace was replaced by loud voices, laughing, shouting and sometimes singing. Where before only birds and animals had been born, lived, and died, now children played in the grass among the trees during the days, and courting couples huddled together and kissed after dark, under the stars.

The road beside the circle of oak trees was no longer wide enough to support the amount of traffic that roared past, as people went to and fro from home to work and back again, and it was full of potholes. This brought more danger to the old oak. In 1962, workmen came and started clearing the fifty foot of ground between the big oak and the old lane surface. The grass was scraped back by JCBs that looked like yellow monsters with giant maws, and the tree felt threatened by this disturbance of the old sod.

Help was at hand though. During the first night of the work, a strange group of people came to the grove. They camped beneath the big tree, putting up rough shelters with tarpaulins and sticks. They rigged them up, complete with sleeping bags, right where the grass had been destroyed, lighting small bonfires and smoking strange smelling tobacco that wafted up aromatically through the night air. They sat in the tree branches, singing together. They brewed tea on the fires and seemed very gentle and calm. They were dressed in pretty, fringed clothes and all of them, even the men, had long hair.

The next morning when the workmen arrived they found their way blocked by the strange group, and they were, understandably to them, furious not to be able to get on with their jobs. They called the protestors a 'bunch of long-haired hippies', and a struggle broke out as the men tried to move them on so that they could start work. The group sat down in quiet protest and refused to be frightened away, even by the heavy machinery. They complained to the foreman that the workmen were destroying half of the big oak's root system with their digging, and making its future uncertain, and they were right.

The leader of the hippies was called Ziggy. He was a lover of peace, of animals and of nature, and he'd become obsessed with trying to make all men respect all that he loved. Ziggy was twenty-seven years old and he had recurrent dreams; nightmares too sometimes. One of the nicer dreams took him to an ancient time and place. He was a man within a tribe and he was strong and fearless. The time he went to was the day that he became 'Father' of the tribe. He would wake up with the feel of the weight of an antlered headdress still on his head, and a feeling of great pride. He remembered a blond girl from the dream, Oriana, and felt a little in awe of her. After that dream he always felt invigorated and empowered. It was quite a shock to wake up in his little bed-sit, with its dowdy wallpaper and cramped little kitchenette, to rediscover who he really was. When he was on one of his protests, as an eco-warrior, he always loved having a group of people around him that looked up to him and followed his lead, just like the tribe had in the dreams. He often wondered if he would one day meet a girl with the unusual name from his dreams, but he never did.

Ziggy looked a bit odd, and was proud of it. He wore his long blond hair natural and curly. He had five earrings in each ear, and a tattoo on the back of his neck of a dove of peace. He only wore clothes made out of natural, unbleached material, like hemp. As he never had much money left over from his giro after his everyday expenses, the clothes were often a bit dirty. Ziggy believed that hemp was the answer to many of the world's problems. You could eat it, wear it, make paper out of it, drive cars fuelled by it, get oil from it, use it for medicine, and, of course, smoke it.

Ziggy would wax lyrical on the subject of his favourite plant to anyone who would listen. Hemp seeds, he would tell them are extremely nutritious. They can be eaten whole, pressed into edible oil or ground into flour for baking. They have very good vegetable protein. They also have in them all the essential amino acids and essential fatty-acids. Hemp is very easy to grow, and can even grow successfully where there is no good soil, or a very short growing season like Scandinavia. But, all the red-tapers and the 'job's worths' could think of, was that a small part of it could be made into a banned drug.

He'd try and tell people that hemp paper is naturally acid-free and because its cellulose level is almost three times that of wood, it makes much better paper, and makes four times the amount of pulp per acre as trees. It's a sustainable, annual crop and is ready for harvest just 120 days after going to seed, compared to trees which take tens or hundreds of years to reach maturity. Further, harvesting hemp doesn't destroy the natural habitats of thousands of distinct animal and plant species. The most important point in all this, to Ziggy, was that hemp could save *trees*, which had to be good news for the planet!

Ziggy was a bit of a crusader in many ways, always joining in the protest marches for peace. This desperate need to stand up and be counted in the name of peace had started with another dream, one that was more of a nightmare. It this dream he would find himself in some kind of deep ditch. He felt like it was a grave. He'd try to climb out but the sides were too steep. When he woke up he always had to look at his finger nails, unable to believe that they weren't caked with mud because he could so clearly remember the very real feel of it forcing its way under his nails as he frantically tried to climb out.

In the nightmare he was always clambering through slimy mud in the bottom of the ditch, almost knee deep in it. Around him were bits and pieces of men, or what had once been men. The mud was smeared with red, mixing in places to a ghastly deep pink gore. That wasn't the worst part though; the worst part was the noise. Bangs and booms of explosions rent the air around him and rattled him down to his soul.

In the nightmare, Ziggy was always screaming, with his hands over his ears, and a man in uniform would always start shouting at him, pointing a gun at him, and always Ziggy knew that he was about to die. The man's words couldn't be heard over the explosive sounds, but his lips moved dramatically, making what he was saying very clear. "Get up! Pick up your weapon! Man the trenches!" Always, Ziggy would be too scared and too frozen with fear to move, and as always the uniformed man's finger could be seen to tighten on the trigger. There was a flash of white light and then just a moment of peace, and Ziggy would wake up. He hated war, violence, any kind of fighting. The very idea of being a soldier made him feel sick with fear. Every time there was a political scare somewhere in the world, he would be filled with dread that war would break out and that he would be forced to go and fight…again.

When Ziggy had opened up to his fellow protestors about his dreams one day, fuelled by the easy influence of several spliffs shared between them, he had discovered to his amazement that most of the peace protestors shared a similar dream, as if once they had all been soldiers caught and terrified in the midst of a war. They all felt the same; that war was evil and that it wasn't right to make young men leave their families and be used as pawns, as cannon-fodder at the whims of politicians. The discussion led to speculation. If past lives were a fact then was it possible that the peace movement these people felt drawn to was their response to having suffered in the trenches, battlefields, warships and planes in the two great wars? The consensus seemed to be that it was highly probable, and this drew the group closer together in their determination to change the world. Other members of the group had different nightmares. Theirs were of the Jewish concentration camps, and of a different but no less evil death and destruction. Some of them had visions of being at a station and being dragged away from their Mothers and Fathers, although in this life nothing like that had ever happened to them.

On this particular protest they knew they couldn't change the whole world, but hoped they might be able to change the world for one small corner of the English countryside. So, now they were at the tree. Ziggy had been guided to the spot by an unusual series of coincidences, which gave even greater meaning to his quest. He'd heard some while back that a new road was being planned while in the nearby fish and chip shop, waiting for his cod and chips. On his way home, a wet newspaper had blown against his legs and he had read the headline, which looked to him like SAVE OLD TREE, but when he'd opened out the sheet, it actually once read, CLOSE SHAVE IN GOLD STREET, and referred to a road accident, the missing letters having been smudged or torn away. Ziggy loved odd things, so he stored the memory away. It didn't take much to put two and two together. Once he was home he saw a local news item on his tiny black and white portable television, while eating his fish supper. It showed the site of the new road. There, standing out like a candle in the dark was a magnificent oak tree. Ziggy had known immediately that the tree was in danger and he had also known exactly what he had to do.

Ziggy discovered that the big tree was one of a circle of seven, and that if this tree that stood alongside the proposed road was damaged then the symmetry of the obviously sacred circle would be ruined too. When he visited the site and the tree, he knew that the place was somehow related to his nice dream, and that he had stood on that spot before, in another life, right next to another tree that had once grown there centuries before. He would stand and hug the big tree and feel what seemed like its heartbeat as its sap rose.

He could also see that by digging for the wider road, they were going to dig up and destroy half of the big tree's root system. He'd quickly gathered a group of his peaceful protestors and they'd set up 'Camp Dru', as they named it, around the tree. It was probably pretty hopeless. It always was, but like always they had to at least try. For some days it looked as if their protest might just be going to work, as the digging was forced to stop, but on the fourth day several cars arrived, and policemen got out. They had brought some vans, and the group were carried bodily into them and driven away. Ziggy's hatred of violence stopped him from taking any more drastic steps against the policemen, but he knew that their involvement would mean that at least the story would get into the local rag, so a few more people would see what was going on.

The workmen shouted derisively after the police vans as they drove off, and then got back to work, gouging into the earth. The tree's tap root took the strain as the smaller lateral roots on the road side were snapped by the mechanical monster that delved beneath them with its big metal teeth. The noisy beast tore up the rest of the grass and the flowers as well as nearly a half of the tree's root system. It was a difficult time for the tree. It was susceptible to disease, and its tap root was loosened in the soil as roots, varying from the thickness of a hair to the thickness of a man's arm, were severed, and pulled, bleeding their juices, from the soil.

Seven times the protestors were released by the police and each time they went right back to the trees. Seven times they returned and tried to stop the work, and seven times they were removed by the police.

Finally, it was over, the men poured their concrete into the big rip in the Earth, and laid their tarmac over the harm they had done the tree. The protestors made new plans, to meet at some other protest site, and disbanded. The road was done, and cars and trucks were free to hurtle along, right under the trees branches, even smashing into those that had grown long, breaking them off and forcing the tree to grow one-sided. Its root system stabilised reasonably well after a while, but it would always have a weakness on the road side, and over time the prevailing winds would gradually start a gentle tilt, so that the tree could no longer quite stand tall and true.

Ziggy still visited the tree occasionally, to apologise to it, and to sit in a dream-state on the grass, leaning against its trunk. He would go off into another world, full of chanting and people he felt at peace with, before returning to a modern day reality that seemed pretty cold and uncaring to him. No-one else really seemed to notice that a beautiful life had been blighted, and that the trees leaves the next year were smaller and less dense as it tried to recover its health after the shock.

# Chapter Nine

Sally didn't call herself a witch, although there were some that would have done, though probably not to her face. There were always enemies and fearful people, when it came to using the old ways. There were also many that loved her and were grateful for the ways she had helped them. Sally would call herself a healer. She'd moved into the overspill housing estate opposite the oak circle, in the late 1960s.

When she did the research that she always did when she moved, she had been saddened to discover that a beautiful, wild forest had been torn down to make way for the houses of the council estate in which she now lived. When she discovered the oak circle a few days after moving in, she had been even more saddened when she sensed that the biggest tree at the head of the circle had been severely damaged when the new road had been laid. Nevertheless she been totally enchanted with the circle, and had adopted it immediately as her outdoor meditation area.

Of course she had to compete for the space with the neighbourhood kids. This was in a time when children played alone or in groups, with never a worry from their parents about 'strangers'. All of the oak trees had suffered many a boy, and the odd girl, scrambling up into their branches, carving their initials, and hammering nails into their trunks to make 'tree-houses'. These usually consisted of one or two planks fixed with bent old nails, to make something slightly more stable for feet to stand on, as high as they dared to climb.

Sally mostly went to the circle late on summer nights, after the children had gone to bed. She'd bring candles and crystals and place them around the tree in a way that pleased her. She would walk around the circle, greeting each tree with respect, like an old and valued friend. Then she would sit on the ground, her back to the biggest and oldest tree. She would close her eyes and breathe slowly and deeply, and gradually she would feel herself start to 'sink' into the tree at her back. She would feel the energy of it soaring upwards through the trunk, cascading into the leaves above and returning into the sky from where it had fallen with the rain. She felt a growing connection with Mother Earth.

She fancied herself as a bit of a medium too, and wasn't surprised when she found that while deep in a trance, she was able to pick up sounds, the odd bit of chanting and the occasional voice, in and around the circle. She could almost hear names among the voices, but just not quite make them out. She didn't think it mattered, because she sensed that the people she was hearing had lived so long ago that there would be no record of them. She also felt a connection to another, long gone member of her craft. She sensed that this woman had come to the same tree many years ago to collect bark and acorns for her mixtures and elixirs.

Sally brought people to the circle for healing. She'd started slowly, with a small meditation circle once a week. It was nothing heavy, just a chance for people who wanted a bit less stress in their everyday lives, and were willing to give up one evening, to switch off and see if they could tap into their intuition. Sally taught her group that meditation was a way they could reconnect with the Earth. The classes were very popular and the people quickly found that they could achieve a wonderful peace from the meditations. Some of them even had visions that gave them answers to questions they had in their everyday lives.

Soon Sally had a group of about fifteen people, varying in backgrounds from a bank manager, through several office and shop workers to housewives. There were only two men in the group, which suited Sally, because she'd found that the women would get intimidated if there were too many men in a group. Luckily the two in hers were also the 'right stuff', calm and non-aggressive.

Once the group were established she got them to practise giving healing energy to each other and many of them said they felt a lot better for it. This was spiritual healing. The members of the group would place their hands above the person they were treating and draw universal energy down through their crown chakras. These are the chakras on the top of the head, the centres for communication with the spirit world or universe. The energy would then be sent down into the patient through the hands, re-energising them so that they could heal their own bodies.

Sally offered individual healing for anyone who wanted it, and she would take those people to the tree circle. She believed that true and full spiritual healing could take place with the help of a mature and sympathetic tree. She felt that if the person who needed healing could achieve close communion with such a tree, they would be able to meld souls with it to some extent and thereby allow the tree to instruct their cells to regenerate, in the same way that the tree's cells could do naturally. Sally believed that we all had that ability, but lost it when we lost our connection to the communal soul of the Earth. Trees can, unlike man or animals, regenerate even if they have been severed to within a foot of the ground, and a whole new tree can grow.

To Sally the Universe and the spirit world were one and the same thing. She believed that our souls returned to communal energy of the universe, and stayed there until they were ready to reincarnate on the physical plane to learn and grow in a way that was only possible as a human, facing everything that goes with that condition. So, to Sally, communicating with the dead simply meant communicating with Universal energy. To her it wasn't necessary to visit graveyards to be with your passed over loved ones, and it wasn't necessary to try and imagine some heavenly place were they might reside. To Sally, all you had to do was look up into the sky.

Sally was also a confirmed 'tree hugger'. She would put her arms as far as she could around a tree and close her eyes. At first all she would be aware of was the rough bark under her fingers, and beneath her cheek, where she rested her face against it, the tree's furry moss coat tickling her nose. Her sense of smell would be heightened and the tree's 'golden' slightly tarry scent would go right to her brain. Then slowly she would start to feel a beat, a throbbing deep within the tree as its sap rose up into the leaves. If the tree was a healthy one this beat would be very strong, especially in the spring and early summer. There was another peak when the fruit was being produced. In the winter, even a strong tree would be quiescent. In a weak tree, at any time it would be fainter, and of course a dead tree would have nothing at all. When she maintained her contact and continued to concentrate she would gradually feel her own energy melding with that of the tree, drawing her into it, allowing their energies become one.

Gradually she would start to feel her senses change and heighten as she became aware of white light she could see with her inner eye, coming from the other trees around the one she was hugging. She would sense the grass at her feet growing, as it quested upwards, and she would feel the flowers as they enjoyed the sun on their upturned faces. After even longer her senses would stretch out like fingertips and start to go deeper into the Earth, so that she could feel the roots of the tree as they burrowed downwards, seeking water. Her senses would start to spread wide and encompass more and more around her, trees, plants and sometimes even animals. She could even occasionally connect to a bird or a squirrel that was above her in the tree, sharing its fears and its hunger or thirst.

Once she achieved a really deep level, whenever she was undisturbed long enough to reach it, her spirit would soar up into the sky, passing through the clouds and the blue, through the atmospheric barrier and into the black of space. She would whirl among the stars there, seeking her own roots and beginnings. We are all made of 'star stuff' and on these occasions, Sally would feel her heart swell with joy as she understood the magnitude of her being. Her spirit would grow and stretch up towards the sun, and she would feel its heat in her soul. She would spread sideways reaching far off galaxies, like a behemoth in an ocean of light.

It was sometimes difficult to come back and break the connection. The hugging always left her emotionally spent and yet refreshed at the same time. She would feel privileged to have been allowed to share another being's energy, and to be carried by it to other realms.

The connection with the planet made her understand her own part in the Universe, and she could never feel alone or abandoned, so long as she had access to a tree spirit. Different trees gave different feelings. A pine tree for instance, seemed to absorb negativity and leave a person feeling fresh and clean. An oak tree would feel strong, dependable and eternal. A yew tree would reach back into the eons of history, taking you with it. A beech tree would fill you with light and joy. An elm would give out nobility and courage.

When one of her group smirked a bit the first time she saw Sally literally hug a tree, the healer asked to be challenged to prove it wasn't nonsense to believe you could 'feel' a tree's life-force. She suggested that she taken into the nearest forest for the test. Soon the group were on a daytrip to Epping Forest. Deep in the trees, Sally was blindfolded and led to twenty-four trees in turn. Without a single mistake she was able to differentiate between the healthy living trees, trees that were obviously diseased, and trees that were actually brown, brittle and dead. The 'smirker' was dumbfounded.

Soon Sally's reputation had spread because she was getting some remarkable results from her method of healing. People started coming from further away, to join her at her special tree for healing. Sally also knew that every living thing on the planet had a part of their soul forever in spirit, and a lot of troubled people could be helped if they were shown how to de-fragment their souls, and reconnect to that powerful part of themselves that resided in spirit. Trees, because they are firmly connected at all times to the communal soul can also help people reach that part of their soul that could help them.

One especially powerful treatment that Sally had devised for ill people was that they should stand and bathe in the water that ran from the oak tree's leaves after a rain shower, or early in the morning, after a frosty night, when the ice was dripping from the branches, or in the spring or autumn, when the dew had been very heavy. After a few years it was not an unusual sight to see quite a crowd of people gathered around Sally and her special tree in the rain, faces upturned, as the pure, clean water dripped all over them.

One day a woman called Sam arrived to have some healing with

Sally. She was an archaeologist and was suffering from recurrent dreams and nightmares. She had even started to have waking visions, which were making her quite afraid. Sam arrived to stay with Sally in the summer of 1986. Sam's nightmares involved her being murdered, and she lived in fear that it was a premonition. The nightmares were starting to rule her life, and affect her work. She also had a lot of problems with her neck and throat, which she put down to stress, but Sally believed the pain and stiffness there was due to something more mysterious than pressure of work.

Sally did several healing sessions on Sam at home, but they didn't seem to work. Sam's nightmares got ever worse, and she would wake up with the taste of a gag in her mouth, choking, and her hands would be grabbing at her own throat, expecting to feel the warmth of fresh blood there. She knew something very odd was going on because with normal dreams or nightmares she would soon forget them, however great the fear at the time. In the light of day any normal nightmare would be shown up as being full of silly fears that melted away in the heat of the sun. These nightmares seemed more and more real, almost more real to her than her waking life, and the fear never faded, only grew.

She started to get really scared to sleep at all, and she also started to get paranoid about walking out alone, in case she was about to be abducted and murdered. Her dreams gradually showed more detail, and she knew that after she was killed she had been buried in a shallow grave. Things got even stranger after that because she had a flashing memory of growing very tall after she died, reaching up to the sky with many arms of different lengths. She even started to think she was going insane.

Sally and Sam grew to be great friends and they would often sit long into the night discussing Sam's dreams over a glass of Sally's elderflower wine. One late spring evening Sally suggested that Sam come and sit in her special place for some healing, by the big oak in the circle. Sam was enchanted by the circle. No other trees had ever managed to grow within the perfect circle of oaks. Instead the grass had grown lush, interspersed with clumps of deep, soft, dark green moss. From the grass peeped the heads of bluebells, and white daisies. Sam was amazed, as was everyone else of Sally's group, by the symmetry of the circle and the beauty of the biggest gnarled oak tree.

However, when she reached out her hands, quite instinctively, to touch the knobbly bark, Sam suddenly drew back, as if she'd been shocked. "Oh!" she gasped, pulling her hands back and then sticking her fingers into her mouth, as if they had been burnt.

"What is it?" Sally asked, anxiously.

"Nothing..." Sam answered, mumbling through a mouthful of fingers. "I don't know. I felt, something sort of creepy, like someone had walked over my grave, and this tingling. I wanted to grab hold of the tree...but I couldn't. It was scary. Oh God, Sally, I really am going bonkers aren't I?" Her eyes filled with tears.

"No, no, not at all. Calm down. This is a sign, a message. This is how 'it' works. We just need to figure it out. This could be the start of all the answers you've been looking for."

Sam looked up, sniffing, her eyes sparkling with tear drops. "Really? You really think so?"

"Yes, I do. Now, just put your hands on the trunk, gradually."

Sam sighed, "Ok, but I don't like it." She reached out gingerly and let her fingertips rest against the trunk.

"Anything?"

"No, it seems OK now…"

"Alright, close your eyes and open your mind. Tell me what you see."

After a few seconds, Sam started to talk, "I see a man carrying a sack. He's putting it on the ground. It's dark…I can't see much. Now he's got a knife…oh!"

Sally reached out to catch her as Sam fell to the ground on her knees. "What is it?"

Sam started sobbing, "It's the same as my nightmare. He's killing me. Oh no! Now I'm having visions while I'm awake!"

It took Sally several hours to calm her friend down. After taking her back to the house and giving her a stiff brandy, she spent ages talking to Sam, telling her that she needn't be afraid, and that she, Sally, was going to sort it all out. She just prayed as she said the comforting words, that she could perform that miracle. She wondered if Sam should see a doctor. It was very odd. People in her group had experienced lots of emotions while at the circle. They'd been ecstatic, peaceful, energised, but not one of them had ever been afraid before.

Over the next few weeks Sam refused to go anywhere near the oak circle. She was in denial that there was anything wrong with her and didn't want to trigger any more symptoms that would shatter her delusion. Sally learned a lot more about her friend. Sam told her that she'd always suffered from nightmares ever since she was a small child, and that she's often scared her Mother by telling her that she sang at night with her 'people'. The nightmares had become steadily worse as she grew into adulthood, whereas it might have been expected that they would decrease.

Sally started researching about nightmares and their causes. She fully believed that most problems people suffered had a spiritual cause, but she was also open-minded to conventional psychology. She felt that she had to be, to safeguard the people she tried to help. She knew that it was believed that there were several reasons for people to be plagued by nightmares; drug-usage, narcolepsy, post-traumatic stress disorder, eating poisonous reef fish, alcohol and fever. She could pretty easily discount the narcolepsy, fever, and eating reef fish. The alcohol and drugs could easily be checked out, and if Sam had been having the nightmares since she was a child, they were unlikely candidates anyway. That left post-traumatic stress syndrome. It was possible Sally thought, that her friend had suffered something awful as a small child that she had suppressed the memory of, so she persuaded Sam to go for hypnotherapy.

Sam agreed, because she was getting desperate and apparently she now had a fear of trees to contend with too! She went for the therapy, and was taken back successfully through her childhood. Several small traumatic incidents were uncovered by the therapist, traumatic to a small child anyway, but nothing that could have caused her to have the nightmares into adulthood. Both women were disappointed, but Sally had another idea. She thought that the trauma might have been carried through from a past life, and she put it to Sam.

The reaction was unexpected. Despite her openness to spiritual healing, Sam was horrified at the idea of investigating her past lives. She snapped back at Sally with, "Don't you think I have enough to worry about in *this* life, without digging up things that might have happened in a past one? Besides, I don't believe in reincarnation. It's a load of rubbish! I've had enough of your hocus-pocus and mumbo jumbo! I'm beginning to wish I'd never come to see you. I'm worse now than I ever was!"

Sally was upset by the reaction, and even more upset when Sam told her that she wouldn't be coming to the sessions at Sally's house anymore, as she was now sure that Sally's treatment had made the nightmares worse. Saying goodbye to the woman she had come to think of as a friend was emotional for Sally. She felt helpless as she watched Sam walk away. She was sure that her treatment had only highlighted the problem, and also sure that Sam was going to be in a lot more trouble before long if she didn't do anything more about the nightmares, which had to be some sort of signs. In her experience, signs were always meant to be followed. Over the coming weeks and then months, she kept expecting to hear from Sam again, but she didn't. She couldn't understand why her mentioning past lives had caused such a negative reaction. It made her even more convinced that Sam's past lives held the answers, answers that Sam was too afraid to face.

# Chapter Ten

Sally kept working with the tree energies at her special circle. Every day she would go down in the evening with a black plastic sack and collect up the debris that had been left there by kids during the day; cans, plastic bottles, sweet wrappers. She'd set out her candles and wait for her patients to arrive. Her circle had become very popular and she had over thirty people in all coming regularly. They didn't all come at once because they would have brought unwelcome attention from the residents of the housing-estate. As it was Sally had found spray-painted insults on her garden fence a couple of times, and no amount of creosote would really cover up the words. It was only kids though, and most people seemed fine about what she did.

The year swung through its cycle and Sally celebrated New Year's Eve 1987 at the circle. She wheeled down barrow loads of small rocks and made a simplistic labyrinth in the centre. She invited her circle to join her and they all took a turn to walk the candlelit maze. It was a time of endings and new beginnings and the labyrinth represented this. Each person walked the paths into the centre and then, after a pause to shake off deadwood from their minds, they walked back out, leaving their baggage behind them, in the centre. Priests of old, Sally explained, used to do the same thing, only they symbolically left the devil behind in the centre. That was why, she told them, that many cathedrals and abbeys have labyrinths carved or painted, within them, or grown from plants outside.

After the walk, the group joined hands around the labyrinth and welcomed in 1987, with joyful, open hearts. At the last stroke of midnight, then turned to each other and hugged. Straw bales then provided the seating, around a log fire, which lit up the overhead branches of the oak circle, making an effective and atmospheric enclosure. The flames and candlelight bounced off the oaks' trunks too, and turned the whole clearing into a magical grotto. They all sat and sang songs until dawn crept in.

That summer Sally hoped she might hear from Sam again, but she didn't call. Sally tried to ring her but Sam refused to speak to her. It filled her with sadness, but also she found that every time she hugged the biggest oak, she would be filled with a need to speak to Sam. Something very strange was going on but Sally had no idea what it could be or what she could do about it.

The spirit of Primrose mourned within the tree and tried many times to speak to Sally. Sam had the way to free Primrose, if she had but known it, and at the same time, she could have freed herself.

The year passed slowly for the oak. This was its three hundredth summer. Something would change this year, and the oak, as always would accept it. The event took place on 16th October 1987. Fifteen million trees would die that night, and the oak would be one of them. The wind got stronger and stronger throughout the night, and in the early hours blue flashes could be seen in the distance as electricity poles and wires crashed down. The tree knew nothing of the cause of the lights, but it felt a shudder within its soul as the wind took hold of its highest branches, still in full leaf. The weightiness of the branches was the biggest problem.

At first the tree was able to resist, but then came the surge. A howling could be heard in the housing estate, coming closer. Branches flew threw the air, propelled from gardens and sent spinning high overhead. This time the tree had no forest to protect it and the wind barrelled between the houses like a wild bull. It tore tiles and corrugated sheets from rooftops and these too became lethal missiles and they sliced through the air on invisible, wind driven wings. Missiles thudded into the oak, chairs, children's bikes, a dog kennel and plastic sheets, mixed in with wooden fence panels that shattered into pieces. The danger to the tree became very real when it felt lateral roots snapping. Because of the road construction it had been left unsupported on its south side, and this was the direction that was sending the wind. Its tap root was embedded many meters into the ground, but it could not hold. As the howling sound reached a deafening crescendo the wind beat a circular tattoo around the oak, twisting it first this way, then that, damaging roots and loosing the whole structure.

The base of the tree shook and shuddered. Then with a terrifying, cracking sound the tap root snapped and the tree staggered. Bereft of its support system the venerable giant started to tilt, further and further, and the more it leaned the faster the lateral roots broke with a sound like a machine gun. The tree fell to the ground, branches shattering and spinning out in giant splinters. The roots tore free from the earth and were lifted into the air just as the branches were dropped to the ground. White bones jangled from the roots that had cradled them like giant hands, and scattered on the ground, falling back into the hole created by the roots being pulled out. Primrose's body was released at last, even though her soul fragment remained trapped within her bones.

The tree lay on its side like a beached behemoth, its roots spiking into the air like questing antenna of some mighty octopus. For a while they quivered with a pseudo life of their own, and then finally stilled, too stiff to be moved by the wind that had felled the tree. The exposed old roots had all been broken off, leaving their live tips in the soil. The tree itself felt the severing of its lifeline, and though it could have survived for some time as it was, it knew somehow that its time had come. It sensed that it would not be replaced in the soil so that it would have another chance, and it started to close down. Life first left the leaves and they became limp, then gradually moisture left the twigs and stems as its roots were unable to draw up any moisture. Finally the spirit of the tree retreated into the heartwood of the trunk, and waited to see what would become of it.

# Chapter Eleven

Sally was one of the first people who emerged into the lessening winds with the dawn. She had been terrified all night, and her worst fear were realised when she saw the oak, a felled titan, looking so surreal, with its roots torn out of the ground, looking like a clutching, multi-fingered hand. She was grief-stricken, and she ran around the huge bulk of the tree, touching its trunk, its branches, it roots, with tears streaming down her face. She finally ended up hugging the trunk on the ground, and was amazed to still feel a connection with it. The tree's spirit continued.

Sally was pleased that the other six trees, being smaller, still stood, albeit with some slight damage, and looked as it they would all survive. After a while, other people, looking shell-shocked, came out of the houses, and some of them walked down to the trees, to gawp at the fallen giant. It was the man from the local shop who first saw the scattered skeletal bones lying in the gaping maw left by the roots.

"My God!" he yelled, "A body! There's a body in there! Bones!"

People gathered around, thrilled somehow by the unfolding drama, still enervated as they were from the night's events.

The police arrived on the scene and screened everything off. It looked as if it would be some while before any clearing of the oak could begin. However, forensics soon discovered that the bones, which were those of an adolescent female, were hundreds of years old, so they did not indicate a recent crime. This made them of little interest to the police and they soon departed the scene, just leaving one officer to await the arrival of the local archaeological representative.

The first thing Sam knew of the incident was when she got an urgent phone call to go to the site of the find. It wasn't until she got quite close that she realised she was going to the very tree that she had feared for years. Her mind wrestled with the battle between doing her job and her fear. Ever since the day when the tree had caused her to have the vision of murder, she had been terrified to return, and so had cut Sally out of her life completely. She decided that she had to go, both to do her job, and to face her demons. It was stupid to go through life afraid of a tree.

Sam wasn't surprised to see Sally waiting outside the cordoned off area surrounding the tree. She walked towards her former friend, a little uncertain as to what reception she might get; after all, she'd been pretty rude to poor Sally, who had only been trying to help her. As she drew closer, she could see the roots and the upper branches of the dreaded tree poking up in a most undignified manner from behind the canvas screens the police had put up, which even now were billowing in the still gusty wind. Sam got close enough to see Sally's face. She was smiling, if a little tentatively. Sam smiled back, and Sally came towards her. They stopped, feet apart. Sally opened her arms and held them out to Sam. Sam rushed towards her and the two women hugged, as if the hiatus in their friendship had never happened.

"Come home," Sally said, her voice muffled by Sam's long blond hair. "Have a cup of tea!"

Sam laughed. Trust Sally to think a cup of tea would cure everything! But as she drew back, Sam said, "Thanks I will. It's been a long journey."

Sally smiled, fully understanding that Sam wasn't referring to the car drive.

"Just give me a second." Sam walked over to the duty policeman and asked him if he would mind waiting while she went and refreshed herself after her drive, and asked him to put her equipment case in the nearby tent, to save her having to lug it to Sally's house and back.

"No problem. Go right ahead," he replied, "I'd sooner be here than clearing up fallen trees and overturned cars any day."

"Thanks, we'll bring you a cuppa back."

Sam followed Sally to her house. They could see the white of the tenting, and the tops of the roots and branches of the oak from Sally's conservatory, where they settled.

Sam sat in a wicker chair with her legs curled up, and something in her started to relax. She knew that scared though she might be, she was at least going to get some answers today. Sally came in with the tea.

"Look, Sally, I'm sorry," Sam began, "I owe you a big apology for things I said."

"No, it's OK, but I wouldn't mind a bit of an explanation. What exactly were you so afraid of?"

"The feeling I had when I tried to touch that tree. There was blood and death, and I suppose I was afraid that I was seeing my future somehow....Do you believe that people can see the future?"

"Yes, I do, but not suddenly like that for no reason, and usually not their own future. You see Sam, psychics – genuine ones that is – have access to the universe on a quantum level. On that level, time is not linear, like we think it is. It runs in parallel lines, so to see the future, or the past, you have to be able to skip across the time lines. Judging by what you saw, I think you may have been seeing the past. I think your nightmares might have been memories, rather than predictions. I don't understand how, but that tree allowed you to see the past – your past."

"That doesn't make any sense, Sally. I'm only 30 years old, and I haven't been murdered, not yet, so if I'm seeing myself, it *has* to be a prediction, doesn't it. What I saw is nothing I have ever experienced."

Sally paused, and then broached the subject of reincarnation again, "Like I said before Sam. I don't think it's *this* life you're seeing."

Sam didn't answer right away. She sipped her tea, hiding her face in the steam that rose from the mug, her blue eyes troubled. Sally took the hint and kept quiet.

After a few minutes Sam looked up from the mug and spoke, "I don't know what's going on, and to be honest if this tree hadn't fallen, and if there hadn't been some archaeological finds underneath it, I probably would have stayed away. It's a bit weird that I keep being brought back here, this time against my will. So...so, I think there is something that has to happen. I have to see this through, whatever it is, and I have to face my fears, and that tree."

"Good." said Sally, firmly. "Right, come on then, let's do it. Let's find out once and for all what the oak tree has to do with you." She stood up, and a bit reluctantly, Sam followed her.

The two women walked down the road toward the felled tree, the grotesque sight of its upturned roots still shocking. As she walked, Sam thought. She hadn't been really happy since she'd walked away from Sally, and the weird stuff. She'd been able to put on a brave face at work in the daytime, but at night, she was pretty much afraid to sleep now. She'd usually end up downing a bottle of wine and nodding off on the couch, only to wake up in the small hours with a headache. She'd slope off to bed and spend the rest of the night toss-ing and turning, her mind ever returning to what she had seen when she touched the tree before. So, it was no good hiding from this, whatever it was. Something had made circumstances where she would find herself at the tree again, and it was time to face her fears and find out what that *something* was.

By then they had reached the policeman, who directed Sam and Sally to the tent where the bones were to be found. Sam didn't know what to do first, get work out of the way and look at the bones, or go down into the root pit and see if there were any other finds to discover, in case it rained again and washed the evidence away or destroyed it. She knew that she should go into the pit, and her hands shook at the thought. She nervously wiped her hands down the sides of her jeans. As if she knew what Sam was thinking, Sally reached out and took her hand. Pulling her gently along behind her, Sally walked to the edge of the root pit.

The hole was vast, somehow obscene, and as they entered it, the roots of the tree became a roof over them. The clouds above scudded across the criss-cross ceiling, and looking up at them Sam got disorientated, feeling as if it was her that was spinning along and the clouds that were standing still. It only added to the surreal feeling that was coming over her. The earth of the sides of the pit were spiky with snapped off roots, some as fine as a hair, others as thick as an arm. The tap root itself, a greenish white stalagmite, had been broken off, and two feet of it stuck out from the bottom of the pit, embedded as it was even deeper into the soil. It was thick and sinewy, and the force required to break it must have been immense.

There were ropes to be used as handholds, and they needed them because the nearer the bottom the more slimy the mud was. In one small corner of her mind, which was still rooted in reality, Sam hoped the countless feet that had climbed up and down the pit hadn't destroyed any evidence there was that might answer the mystery of the bones. The rest of her mind was quaking in some other world. Both women slithered and slid to the bottom of the pit. Sam started work, forcing her professionalism to lead her. It soon became obvious that there was not much to find. There were some muddy scraps of material. Some of it looked like sacking and some had a fine print and was some kind of cotton. Sam always had a supply of plastic bags with labels on in her coat pockets and she carefully collected all the scraps she could, bagged them and wrote on the labels, while Sally stood to one side, out of the way.

Sam felt her back brush against the tap root, and she reached around instinctively to push it away. Her hand grabbed it, feeling with distaste the slight sliminess of it, and then she was whirled instantly into another time and place. She was lying on the ground, shaking with the freezing cold, and a knife was flashing towards her throat. She tried to scream but her mouth was full of wadded rags. She could see a man above her wielding the knife. He was dirty, evil and terrifying. The knife slashed at her bare throat and it closed in terror as warmth flooded down her chest. Her throat found air at last and she did manage to scream, opening her eyes to find Sally bending over her anxiously.

The policeman's head appeared, peering over the side of the hole. "Everything alright?" he asked.

"Yes," Sally answered quickly, "It's pretty muddy down here. She slipped."

"Grab the rope," the Constable replied, "I'll give you a hand up."

Sam clutched at the rope, grasping it so tightly that it hurt her hands. It was all she could do not to panic completely and scramble out of the hole in such a demented way that the policeman would have probably called for an ambulance. While Sam might feel ready to be tranquilised and locked up, she was damned if she was going to let it happen. She managed to climb out reasonably calmly, although her back prickled with the feeling that something was going to grab her and drag her back down into the pit. She could see in her mind's eye, the tree roots, like a demonic hand, coming to life and grabbing her in its giant fist. By the time she reached the top she was shuddering.

Sally was soon standing beside her, and Sam looked back down into the pit with her friend's arm about her for support. "OK?" she asked.

"I'm alright," Sam replied, "But I'm sorry Sally, I'm never touching that damn tree again no matter what you say!"

"OK, maybe there's another way. Don't worry about it for now, just get the job done and we'll go and have some lunch. I'll go and wait for you indoors. Um...you *will* come and find me won't you?"

"Yes, I won't do another runner on you, I know you're only trying to help me, and I missed you." She hugged Sally, and the healer walked off towards her house, patting the tree trunk sadly as she passed it by.

# Chapter Twelve

Minutes later, Sam sighed as she entered the police tent. The bones were laid out on a table. Sam added the scraps of cloth to items on the table, placing them carefully into trays so that they could be examined and dated later. She turned to the bones. It was an entire skeleton, and although the bones had broken apart, they had been laid out in their correct positions and relationships with each other. It was most unusual, Sam thought, to find bones all together like this one, unless they had been carefully buried. It looked like there might have once been a burial site where the trees now stood. This meant there should be other bones to find nearby.

She read the police report before continuing. It told her that the body had been found broken apart by the roots. That it appeared as if the roots had actually been entwined around the bones; a macabre thought. The team had also found evidence in the then undisturbed mud at the bottom of the pit, which indicated that the body had originally been placed in the ground in a foetal position. This tied in with other ancient burial rituals, but didn't tie in with burials carried out at the age of these bones. Sam hadn't known the age given until she read the report. For the body to have been buried without any kind of coffin, and on non-sacred ground, it a foetal position, the bones would have had to have been at least hundreds of years older. Sam realised for the first time since she had got the email telling her of the find that she was probably looking at a murder victim.

Deciding not to wait for backup and confident in her own ability, now that professional curiosity had washed away her shivers from her encounter with the awful tree, Sam got ready to examine the bones. She put on a plastic apron and some rubber gloves, got out her microscope and set it up. She took out a number of rigid plastic trays with pop on lids, so that she could carefully label and store the bones, ready to transport them back to the museum for further analysis.

Her mind now tightly focused on the job that she adored, Sam reached out and gently picked up the skull. She gazed into the empty eyes. Suddenly her mind zipped away again. She was no longer standing in the tent, instead she was outside, and it was night-time. It was frosty, freezing cold, and she could see white breath pluming from the mouths of the people that stood all around her. She looked down at Gildas. A tear slid unbidden from her eye, and she quickly sniffed it away, because this was a time of rejoicing, not mourning. Gildas was leaving his sick old body and going to walk with the stars. She would miss his presence and be a little sad without him and his wisdom, but that was her hurt, not his. To be too sad about his leaving would be selfish. She smiled at him.

She looked around at her people. It was time for her to choose a new leader. This wouldn't be her first time. Once before the 'Father' of the tribe had been killed out hunting, and another time, another 'Father' had died from disease. Gildas would be the last one she saw leave, she was sure of it. Several young men looked back at her hopefully, but there was one older man who had been passed over before. She looked at him, and saw not just his body but the aura of his spirit. It was a clear blue, the colour of honour and purpose. He shone like a beacon. It was time for Druce to take his rightful place as Father of the tribe. Oriana's eyes held his for a moment, and she nodded. Druce stepped forward eagerly.

Between them, Oriana and Druce collected all the messages for the Goddess, taking them from Gildas' shaking hands, and hung them on the lower branches of the biggest yew tree. Oriana knelt down beside Gildas and put her hand on his head. She started to speak to him, but the man in front of her suddenly vanished and she found herself looking up at the night sky in puzzlement. She couldn't move her arms or legs and her mouth was stuffed with rags, and gagged. A man hovered above her and a knife flashed down. Primrose, as she now knew herself to be, was washed in warmth, and a part of her floated up, up and up, towards a bright light in the sky. Back on the ground another part of her felt left behind, as if the suddenness and trauma of her death was somehow holding her back.

All was dark as Sam's awareness stayed with this earthbound fragment of Primrose's soul. Then light started to permeate the darkness. She felt enveloped in armour, safe and secure, but through a grainy surface she could sense daylight, the sun, the rain. This facet of her was trapped, but it was safe and for now it felt content. This was a special part of Primrose.

Sam raced back suddenly to awareness of herself. She involuntarily took a deep breath and something entered her with the air she drew in. She opened her eyes, she was unafraid, and she felt a sense of completeness that she only now realised had been missing for all of her life. She felt whole.

Sam gasped, there were tears in her eyes and suddenly she knew what was going on. She knew what her nightmares had been about, and she knew that she had been Oriana, and Primrose, and probably others in between. Reverently Sam placed Primrose's skull into one of the plastic boxes and packed it carefully with bubble wrap. She couldn't wait to talk to Sally about it all, and she rushed from the tent, quite ignoring the startled look on the policeman's face as she raced past him. She hurried on up the road and into Sally's garden by the back gate, knowing instinctively that she would find her friend in the conservatory.

Sally looked up, concerned for a moment at her friend's sudden entrance, but then smiled as she took in the expression of total wonderment on her face. There was no doubt this was good news at last.

Sam told her everything, very excitedly, finishing with, "So, you were right all along Sally. It wasn't the tree that was out to get me at all, it was *me!* Me from a past life, trying to communicate with me."

"And that doesn't scare you anymore?" Sally asked. "The idea of having lived before?"

"No, it's weird, but as soon as I was Oriana I just knew everything. Even when Primrose was being killed I wasn't scared, because I knew it wasn't the end. How could it be when I had already been someone else?"

"It's wonderful!"

"There's one thing I don't get though. I don't understand what happened to Primrose. I felt one part of her going to…to 'walk with the stars', but another part was trapped, and that was the part that's been calling to me all this time. She needed me to help her…escape…but from where?"

"I'm not sure. Let me think about it. Where did you think that part of her was?"

"It was like being alive, but not. Behind a wall, a wall made of energy, so I could sort of see through it, but not quite."

"Oh, wait, I see. You said that Oriana believed Gildas was going up to the stars through the yew tree?"

"Yes, that's right. To the Goddess."

"Well, then maybe Primrose was doing the same thing, but a part of her was afraid, traumatised by suddenly dying so violently and terrifyingly. Maybe that small part wouldn't leave the Earth. It stayed in the tree, sort of trapped there after a while, until you came along, and was willing to listen long enough for her to…sort of latch back onto you."

"But I didn't listen, I couldn't listen. And maybe I have been back since in other lifetimes and not listened then either. If the tree hadn't come down…If I hadn't been brought into physical contact with Primrose's body…Oh Sally, do you suppose…? Is it possible that the oak tree sacrificed itself to set her free?"

"Yes, it could be, maybe it could be. Or if not the tree consciously, maybe some other…force…decided to sacrifice it."

"And all this time I hated that tree."

"Never mind. This has confirmed something for me. I always had a theory about ghosts, some ghosts anyway. I think that whenever we leave a life traumatically and suddenly, a part of us can get left behind, like with Primrose. I think sensitive people can sense those fragments, and believe them to be ghosts. I bet some people thought that tree was haunted. I think I sensed Primrose myself. Then, if we go to that place, where we once died, the fragment can be absorbed back into us, and hey presto – no ghost anymore."

# Chapter Thirteen

Sam worked tirelessly to try and solve the mystery of Primrose's death, feeling that it was unfinished business she had come back to clear. She had some sessions with a hypnotherapist and discovered the right year and her surname, Lawrence. As the girl had been killed reasonably close to home, Sam was able to find a report of a missing girl who never came home, and it was Primrose Lawrence. She never knew exactly why Primrose had been murdered, or who had done the killing, but it was enough to lay her to rest. Sam wondered if maybe one day she would find Primrose's parents reborn, and if she did, whether they would still be suffering from the trauma of not knowing what had happened to their daughter. *My God,* she though, *so many ills and problems could be resolved by finding out what happened in past lives.*

Sam had suffered from neck and throat problems all her life. She got sore throats and coughs at the drop of a hat, and couldn't shift them for weeks. She couldn't bear anyone to touch her neck, so seeing a doctor about the sore throats was always an ordeal. The very thought of ever having to submit to surgery in that area, for any reason, was enough to give her a panic attack and cold sweats. Even in the height of summer she couldn't relax unless she had something high around her neck. She would often have to wear a silk scarf, or if even that made her too hot and itchy, a many stranded choker necklace could help.

Solving the mystery was also enough to cure Sam once and for all, of the painful and inconvenient problems that she had always suffered from. Her sore throats seemed to be a thing literally 'of the past', and at last she was able to wear scoop necked T shirts without feeling vulnerable. Sally told her that this was often the case with past life healing. People often suffered from some kind of injury or disease that was related to how they had died traumatically in the distant past. It was also possible, Sally told Sam, that if she hadn't opened herself to her past, she might have actually developed a serious throat condition that would indeed have entailed the dreaded surgery. The surgeon's scalpel would literally have been recreating the wound that killed Primrose. Sally believed that illnesses and diseases often had their roots buried deep in the past.

Sam also knew instinctively that poor Primrose had tried to connect with her in many other incarnations, but that in the end the only way for her to break through was for her body to be revealed and a direct physical connection made with Sam. Even that wouldn't have worked in any other lifetime, because unless she was a police officer, or an archaeologist, as Sam was in her current life, she still wouldn't have come into close contact with it.

Sam came to realised that the universe does indeed work in mysterious ways, and that her lifetimes since being Primrose were pointers and signpost and eventually a route map for her to be in the position to connect with her previous self. She came to understand that there were beings whose quest it was to give people these signposts and manoeuvre them into the right positions to 'wake them up'. She called these beings 'past life' or 'soul' angels and understood how they worked, travelling right next to us through life after life and death after death, helping us and guiding us to wake up to our spiritual being.

Sam's life was changed in many ways by her wake up call. As well as her terrible nightmares, which she now knew were memories and her neck pain going, she had always had other problems. Even as a small child she had amused and yet worried her parents by being too adult. She had not played like other children, but had been obsessive with her toys, not enjoying playing, but wanting everything to be ordered and serious. As she'd entered her teenage years she'd developed a weight problem, and she would eat even though she wasn't hungry. For years she'd hated what she saw in the mirror, but had seemed powerless to do anything about it. She'd had problems finding a secure relationship. This was because she was afraid of men. It took a long, long time for her to trust a man, and this was often too long for the young men she met. They didn't have the patience to wait for her.

Sally explained to Sam that the age Primrose had died at had clues to Sam's problems. The fact that Primrose's childish excitement at eavesdropping, and her sense of adventure, had directly caused her death as she saw it, had made Sam repressed in that area. Once she had reconnected with Primrose, it was as if she'd reunited with her carefree, childish hopes and imagination, as well as a sense of daring. A part of her that had been missing returned, and Sam was much happier because of it.

Her weight started to drop off, because as the regressionist told her, anyone who has been killed suddenly by a sharp blade in a past life is liable to be overweight deliberately. This made a lot of sense, after all a thin person is much more likely to die from a stab wound than a fat one. Sam found out that obese people often carry the excess weight as protection, armour against a sudden knife attack. Within a few months Sam had dropped three stone. She knew also that her problem with relationships would fade. It was obvious that her fear of men came from the one who had abducted and murdered her. Healing sessions, taking her past her death in that life and allowing her to look back on it from a position of spirit, would soon have her reacting rationally to men.

The only downside was that the tree had been killed by the hurricane.

Sam had a new quest. She knew on a deep level that the wonderful oak tree, the tree that she had feared and hated, had been sacrificed to bring her peace in her life. It still lay where it had fallen. She was now very concerned about what was to become of it. She'd gone back to the tree several times with Sally, and they were both convinced that even though the tree was obviously dead in a physical sense, there remained a spirit within it. They both felt it when they touched the tree. Whether it was because it had housed part of a human soul they didn't know, but for some reason the tree spirit seemed reluctant to leave. So, the two of them couldn't bear the thought of the tree just being chopped up and destroyed. Of course it had to be moved. They didn't want it to just lie there and rot; they wanted it to have a chance to continue experiencing things. After all, it was said that all our souls started as trees, and if that were so then this one was more advanced than most. So they sat up for several nights, sipping hot cocoa and counting the stars, and talking about what might be the best thing for it.

Luckily it would be a few weeks more before workmen might be sent to clear the tree. It wasn't lying across any cars or electricity wires, or anyone's property, so it wasn't a priority. There were thousands more trees to be cleared that were causing problems. Then they found out that the tree would most likely be cut up into manageable pieces and used for hundreds of different things. They didn't want that to happen, they wanted the 'heart' of the tree to remain in one piece. If it had stayed where it was, it would have certainly supplied homes and food for a myriad of creatures, but if they could think of a way to preserve it, to keep the spirit of the tree alive, that would be better. Also, if the tree was cleared, it would make way for a new one to grow in its place, and thereby retain the circle of seven.

They heard of a man called Jeremiah Pogue who specialized in carving large portions of trees into useful objects, often using nearly the entire trunk in one piece. They went to meet him, in his lonely but peaceful cottage. Prejudging him from his rather archaic name, they expected to find an old, wizened man, but he was young, only in his twenties. Jeremiah was an interesting man with controversial views, and he certainly had an old head on young shoulders. It was very strange that such a young man should have developed such wonderful skills as a craftsman, and also that he would be so self-assured and firmly fixed onto his pathway.

He despised organized religions, calling them the 'root of all evil'. He claimed that for the sake of man's spiritual evolution, we should turn our backs on all religions. He thought that while there would always be good men doing good deeds, and evil men doing evil deeds, only religion created situations where good men could be persuaded to do evil things. As he spoke to her Sam got a strange feeling. She felt very strongly that she had known Jeremiah before. As his words were spoken, in her mind's eye, she saw not the modern day, youthful, clean-shaven craftsman, but another man. He was grey-haired and bearded. He was a leader among men, and his name was Gildas. Sam didn't say anything, but she smiled a secret smile and enjoyed the reunion.

Jeremiah told them that the local people had been asking for a footbridge over the stream that ran across a footpath, a quarter of a mile away, and this seemed like it might be the perfect solution. To Sam and Sally's delight the local council agreed, probably only too happy to have one fallen tree problem taken care of. Jeremiah was very keen to help them with the tree. Sam was happy to pay for the removal, and she and Sally watched as the massive trunk was first cut through, severing it from the branches and making a flat end. The same was done at the root end, and then the entire trunk was split right down the centre, and dragged to the stream.

Jeremiah supervised the positioning of the trunks across the watercourse, anchoring them firmly at each end with stakes cut and shaped from the branches of the tree. He painstakingly carved more branches into handrails, and finally the bridge was complete. Anxiously, Sam and Sally went to see the footbridge. They were very happy with how it looked. The whole bridge had the appearance of something that had grown there naturally. Jeremiah had done a great job, but one thing remained. They placed their hands on the trunk, and they were delighted to immediately feel the energy that was still within the wood.

A small opening ceremony was held, and a group of local people waited to cross the bridge for the first time. Jeremiah declared the bridge, 'open' and a photographer from the local paper took a photo of the people walking across it.

Happy that the tree would live on, to experience more of life through the people and animals that crossed it, Sam and Sally left it to its new life. They talked as they walked, and wondered whether one day, perhaps in hundreds of years' time, the tree's soul would be housed within a human body. It was possible they decided, because all souls had to start somewhere. They agreed that if it was going to happen, then the tree's soul would make a wonderful and wise person.

The stream glistened and burbled beneath the oak, flashing in a golden sprinkling of afternoon sunshine, traced by the leaves that were still on the surrounding trees. Birds were singing, and there was not the slightest sound of a car or a train or any machinery. The breeze gently soughed through the dry and bronzed leaves of the autumn-clad beech trees in the wood.

Later in the day, when the people had dispersed and all was still, a red squirrel emerged from the near silence. Rare in those parts by then, the little animal bounced across the prone trunk, pausing half-way, his round, black eyes flicking this way and that, seeking warning signs of danger. Seeing none, he stood upright, his bushy tail curled up over his back as he cocked his head. His fluffy ears twitched, as if he was listening to something. He stayed that way for several moments as he chattered to himself as if in satisfaction, and then finally he scampered across to the other side of the stream and vanished into the woodland beyond.

Twilight gradually stole over the bridge and the moon appeared, bright and splendid at her fullest. All the birds were silent except for a lone barn owl that made the occasional screech as it silently floated on the moonlight. The moonlight hovered over all, turning the water silver and the bronze leaves, platinum. Bats whirled through the darkness, almost blind and yet able to see. A deer delicately picked its way down to the stream. She sniffed and snorted suspiciously at the bridge because it was new, but soon realised that there was nothing to fear. The tree's spirit was at peace in its new role.

The next day, a little girl of nine years old walked up the footpath to the bridge with her mother and father following a few steps behind her. She stopped and stood still, apparently enchanted at her first sight of the bridge, calling back to her mother that the bridge was full of fairies who were crossing over.

Then she too stopped, as if listening. "Mummy!" she cried, "I can hear someone singing!" She giggled, and her feet pattered on the timber as she ran across. She gambolled off, following the sounds that only she could hear.

This spirit of the tree would live for many more years. Just as it had experienced fragments of the lives of hundreds of people who had passed by it as a tree, so the bridge would do the same with the thousands of people who would walk across it. Some people, those who were aware of the secret world that marched alongside their own, would hear sounds as they crossed the bridge, and wonder.

Back at the circle, the ground where the tree had stood looked empty and forlorn for months. The root pit had been filled in after the archaeologists had finished, and the earth was smooth and flat. Sam and Sally walked past the patch often, saddened by the gap that was still so obvious.

Then on one such walk in the following spring, Sam suddenly stopped next to the patch, a big smile on her face. "Oh my God," she whispered.

"What is it?" asked Sally, puzzled.

"Look," answered Sam simply, pointing.

There on the ground, pushing its way up through the surface was a tiny sapling. It was a fledging yew tree. Where it had come from was a mystery, because the women knew there were no yew trees nearby. By some magic known only to Gaia, the circle was about to be completed again.

# Epilogue

Every form of religion and belief system, even the newest, has its roots in the oldest, in a time when the sacredness of plants, and trees in particular, was universal. These wonderful planetary guardians are much more than meets the eye.

Trees communicate with each other. In a forest if one tree is attacked by beetles for instance, that tree will produce a substance that is distasteful to the beetle, and all the other trees, whilst at that point beetle-less, will produce the same substance in anticipation of attack.

Worship of nature was considered as paramount for centuries. Even today you would have to be a spiritually devoid person if you were not humbled by the towering majesty of a 300 year old oak tree; alive before your birth, and living well beyond your death. The older religions, such as Paganism, embraced the conception of the unity of life in nature, and accepted that our future was intrinsically entwined with that of trees. How right they were. Now that we see the folly of destroying rain forests and thereby severely compromising the green 'lungs' of the planet, maybe we can comprehend the 'common sense' aspects of the old ways.

Roman historians seem to have been among the first to comment on the Celts' love and respect for their sacred groves, speaking of them as the centre of their whole religion. Some of the tribes took the names of trees as their own; hence *The Men of Oak, The Sons of Yew,* and *The Rowan Men.* The Celts believed that each tree had a spirit or dryad inside it. The saying *knock on wood,* came from a belief that knocking on a tree would awaken the dryad within. Dryads come in male and female form; these are more commonly known as Luna and Sola trees and the personality of each dryad reflected the nature of the tree it resided in.

### Yew

A sign of the circle of life, and inspired hope in the possibility of rebirth and regeneration.

### Apple

This tree possessed an aura of youthfulness and innocence.

### Blackthorn

This tree and the dryad within was thought to be protected by fairies. Anyone who harmed a Blackthorn tree was in danger of revenge from the spirits.

### Gorse

This tree contained the energy of fertility, and the dryad within was as mischievous as a child.

### Poplar

Symbolizing strength and courage.

### Mistletoe

Whilst not an actual tree, but a symbiotic growth often found on other trees, this shrub was associated with birth and new beginnings, adventurous and innovative.

## Beech

If the oak was the King of the forests, then the beautiful beech with its golden autumn tresses must have been the Queen. It stood for stability and balance.

## Elm

Symbolized the dark side of the psyche, and therefore its dryad was to be feared and respected.

## Hazelnut

Feeder of many in the winter months the hazelnut brought a sense of elation and exhilaration

## Sycamore

Often growing in unlikely and apparently barren places, this tree therefore came to indicate perseverance and vitality.

## Birch

Especially beloved of Druids, the spirit of the birch represented new life.

## Rowan

The berries of the rowan were believed to be the food of the Gods, and therefore most sacred. Woe betide anyone who tried to harm this tree or its dryad.

## Ash

The tree of enchantment. Many were the poor peasants lured and bewitched by the power of the ash dryad.

## Alder

Anyone who destroyed this tree and the home of its resident dryad would be held responsible for any crisis that befell his village.

## Hawthorn

What would today be considered a humble tree was once imbued with the secret of everlasting life. So, this tree which today is wantonly destroyed would in the past have been revered and protected.

## Oak

Used in many ceremonies, believed to protect from lightning, and the very essence of the circle of life, the oak tree was the true King of trees, and its dryad equally powerful.

## Holly

Because it is evergreen, the holly tree symbolized the true eternal nature of Mother Earth.

## Elder

Believed to contain the very spirit of the sun, this tree was as protected as life itself was defended.

That other ancient and spiritual race, Vikings, held religious beliefs that were firmly attached to trees. It's written that their God, Odin said, "I know that I hung on the windswept tree. The wisest know not from whence spring the roots of that ancient tree." This refers to his Shamanic journey, from which he emerged with gifts from the 'other' reality, one of which was the runic language. (Still used today as the symbols on Runes). The tree itself was thought to represent a ladder into the 'above', from whence all knowledge came. Odin is said to have remained in the tree for nine days and nights without food or water. This deprivation, as with Jesus in the wilderness, transported him into other realms of consciousness.

Odin saw a huge ash tree in his trance state. It was so immense that its branches encompassed the whole world and beyond. The tree supported three disks; the Upper World, the Middle World and the Lower World, and one can still see the influence of this in the propensity of threesomes in modern religion. There is Heaven, Hell, and Purgatory; likewise the trio of the Father, Son and Holy Ghost. It seems that there are often three levels in belief structures.

In the folklore of most primitive people, like the Aboriginals of Australia, scared hunting locations were marked by distinct trees, as well as rivers and large rocks. These people believed that there was a deep and spiritual connection between them and the natural elements that surrounded them. These people were hunter-gatherers, but even in the more advanced cultures of agricultural man, sacred groves played a huge part.

In the ancient world, Slavic people also revered woodland spirits and built sanctuaries among the oldest and most sacred tree groups. They too believed that spirits lived in the trees and so would never cut them down for fear of displeasing those that dwelt within. Once separate peoples starting growing closer together as their populations expanded, these same special places were used as sites where different tribes could join together to worship.

In Greek and Roman times, the countryside was speckled with hundreds of enclosures, used for sacred purposes, and such was their proliferation that they did in fact take up much of the land. Each one would contain a group of trees and a spring. These places were kept natural, all forms of interference forbidden. A 1st century philosopher said, *If you come upon a grove of old trees that have lifted up their crowns above the common height and shut out the light of the sky by the darkness of their interlacing boughs, you feel that there is a spirit in the place, so lofty is the wood, so lone the spot, so wondrous the thick unbroken shade.*

Ovid is quoted as saying, *Here stands a silent grove black with the shade of oaks; at the sight of it anyone could say, 'there is a spirit here!'* Virgil is known to have said, *Some God has this grove, the Gods favour wild trees unsown by mortal hand.* So the people believed that the very naturalness of the trees pleased the Gods, and that they should not be interfered with. Some of them were huge; for instance the grove of Daphne was ten miles in circumference. The Goddess Artemis had an entire island left in its wild and natural state in honour of her.

The Greeks also were proactive in their protection of all wildlife and plants – trees in particular, and the Goddess Artemis would have been furious and would wreak revenge on any people who destroyed her 'garden'.

In early Africa the fig tree was held as sacred. It was forbidden to use axe or fire against this tree, and even wildlife that resided in or around these trees could not be hunted; confusingly though goats and sheep were often sacrificed in the same sacred area. It was also believed that the weather could be controlled by the spirits that lived in the trees, and that they also had healing power.

Often the sacred groves, protected by the Mbeere tribes would be up to three hectares, and some were still around thirty or forty years ago. It was terrible taboo to damage a single branch of one of these trees, nor was it permitted for even the fallen branches to be used as firewood.

The ancient Egyptians worshipped trees and depicted them in their temple architecture, and trees were also an integral part of the belief systems in Arabia, Persia, Assyria, Britain, Scandinavia, China, India, Ceylon and many other parts of the world.

In Indonesia the banyan tree, *Ficus benghalensis,* is considered sacred. The natives believe that holy spirits live in the trees and keep the springs, which often accompany them, clean and safe to drink. The Javanese also believe that sacred spirits dwell deep within forests.

The Tree of Life is the central feature of Kabbalah. According to its teachings, the Tree of Life was put into place before Creation. Everything in Creation is patterned after the Tree of Life. The ten spiritual centers or *Sefirot* in the Tree of Life represent the ten Divine attributes of God within man.

So why did the sacred groves disappear from Europe? One reason is that anything of possible Pagan origin was considered devilish and therefore destroyed. The emperor Theodosius II (5th century AD) issued an edict directing that the groves be cut down unless they had already been appropriated for some purpose compatible with Christianity. This is why you will often see a gigantic tree in a churchyard or monastery – these are the ones that were spared, because the Christian trappings were built beside them, thus cleansing them of their supposed satanic connections.

A greater population required more timber for buildings and fuel; agriculture took up all the available land, and the groves fell victim to the axe. Of course centuries ago forests were replanted in order to appease the hunting appetites of various royal houses, but most who believe in the sanctity of trees also believe that the Gods prefer natural rather than contrived growth. However, at least this planting, for whatever motive, means that we do still have some ancient trees.

Tree-huggers are often pooh-poohed by modern day people, but anyone who seriously tried it can't fail to be affected, if they just give it an open mind. A suitable tree – one which draws you will welcome you into it. If you meditate with physical contact with the tree, you will feel its great energy as it rises with the sap, especially in spring or early summer. The tree's energy – especially in a tree that has been there for many centuries longer than you – will calm you and fill you with a connection to the planet. Various trees give of different energies.

**Ash:** Brings peace of mind.
**Beech:** Helps to balance mental health.
**Cedar:** Cleanses negativity.
**Oak:** Brings a feeling of well-being.
**Pine:** Revitalises you if you are worn down.
**Willow:** Helps communicate with someone who has passed over.

If you would like to try a spot of tree-hugging, first go to a quiet group of trees; preferably ancient woodland, stand still and find silence in your mind. Breathe deeply and concentrate on 'feeling' the energies that surround you. When you are ready, walk through the trees, and as you enter the aura of each one, ask if that tree is the right one for you. When you find the right one, reach out to it carefully, seeking the tree's agreement to the contact with you. Wrap your arms around the trunk and let your head rest against the bark. After a few seconds you may feel a soft vibration inside the tree, which is its life force. Reach into the tree with your spirit and bathe in the stream that rises up in the centre.

Sometimes you will start to see the world around you from the tree's perspective, and you will start to notice the auras of the other trees around you, as sensed by your tree. If you can achieve it this is a remarkable and emotive experience. But beware; it may change how you perceive the world around you forever, an awareness that will bring you a sense of huge responsibility at the same time.

Move gently away from the tree when you are finished, with consideration, for the tree will have been sensing your energy too. Thank the tree, as you should always thank nature for giving you a beautiful experience, whether it be a rainbow, a sunset or just a wonderful view.

People have even tied in specific trees to your personality, so if you're drawn to a particular tree, have a look and see how that ties in with your own personality – and if it matches and you're looking for a tree to hug – this might be the way to do it.

### APPLE

You are gracefully made and very charming and attractive. You have a great sense of adventure, but always need genuine love in your life. You are a gentle yet passionate and true lover. You also have a great imagination and a real sense of philosophy.

### ASH

This tree belongs to an outstandingly attractive person, full of élan, impulsive and exciting. However, you are a very demanding person. Intelligent and daring, inclined to take chances, you are also a little vain, but despite this you are someone who takes relationships very seriously.

## BEECH

You are a very creative person, with good taste, but a little over concerned about your appearance. You are not a risk-taker, but you do enjoy sport. You are a good partner to choose if someone wants to settle down

## BIRCH

If this tree attracts you, you are someone who shies away from excesses of all kinds. You prefer moderation, and although an attractive person to others, you are unassuming. You aren't a very passionate person, but you bring an aura of calm to any situation

## CEDAR

You are beautiful, but you do know it. Not one to hide your light you will go for a life of luxury. You tend to be impatient and be very decisive. You have many talents and are not afraid to use them to get what you want. You are a success but tend to yearn for something 'unknown'.

## CHESTNUT

Another beautiful person on the physical level, but you care more about others than yourself. You are a little over-sensitive, but very tactful and able to mediate. Not very confident, you often hide this by going a little too far in the other direction and can give people the wrong impression. They will sometimes find you over-assertive, not realizing that this is an act.

## CYPRESS

You are physically strong, of good stature, and you are very happy-go-lucky. It would take a lot to faze you. You need a partner because you hate your own company, but that's good because you have great passion and are faithful – a rare combination. You can however, be a little clumsy.

## ELM

You are a great friend! Noble to the extreme and you often make sacrifices for others. You don't ask much for yourself but you don't suffer fools gladly, and you would rather be a leader than a follower. You have a great sense of fun and are a trustworthy partner, although you do tend to think you know what's best for others.

## FIG

You are very reliable, but you tend to be a bit stubborn. You are gregarious and love nothing more than to be within a group of friends. You hate others arguing, but are a great home-maker, treating all in your family circle with love. You might be a bit of a practical joker.

## FIR

You can appear a bit enigmatic and sometimes you have an uncertain temper. You are sophisticated and love to be surrounded by quality. You can be discontented with one partner and you have many friends who love you for your reliability, but also many enemies who can't handle your independent spirit.

## HAZELNUT

You're everybody's friend, a real charmer. You are a good listener and you make a very good first impression. You are a trustworthy and honest partner, but you can have flighty moments. You need a partner who can tolerate you flirting, whilst understanding that it's just your way. You are a very good judge of character.

## HORNBEAM

You are very fastidious – probably a Virgo. You love comfort and pampering. However, you're not over proud and you like to find kindness and discipline in others. You can mistrust others and be quick to make snap judgements of them. You don't like making decisions as you are a perfectionist and hate the idea of getting it wrong, which makes you appear indecisive.

## LIME

You often complain and are quick to become jealous if you don't get your partner's undivided attention. You hate arguments and hard work, but you have many talents. They can go unused because you find it hard to get motivated. You think that what will be, will be, whether you try or not. You are a fiercely loyal friend.

## MAPLE TREE

An exceptional person. You have an odd mixture of being shy but self-confident at the same time, often confusing others. You love adventure and are brave and resourceful. You will often have a photographic memory and can't understand why others find tests difficult – you devour the challenge.

## OAK

Tough and uncompromising, you make a very bad enemy. Luckily you don't have many, because people are drawn to your strength and charisma. You are never flighty; pragmatic and sensible; your feet are always grounded. You tend to act while others are still thinking, which can intimidate them.

## OLIVE

The lover of this tree is a wise person. You will always prefer to live in a hot country. You will talk rather than fight and you're very good at it. You are very tolerant and would make a good diplomat. You are never envious or jealous, you are sensitive and happy. People love to be around you, as you uplift them without even trying.

## PINE

You have many acquaintances but few really close friends. You feel nervous and expect to be cheated on if you let people get too close. But once someone becomes a friend you will go through hell or high water to protect them. However, if someone makes an enemy of you, you will be equally dogged and they will live to regret it. You are disappointed in people who don't keep promises.

## POPLAR

You are not very confident, but you should be! Other people see the true you where you have only self-doubt. You don't like to fight, but if forced into one you will be brave and stand your ground. You are creative and love organizing things; you are reliable and philosophic. Once you find your partner you stick like glue through thick and thin.

## ROWAN

You love to be the centre of attention. The limelight holds no fears for you, and it's your natural place. You hate to be still and are always looking to the horizon no matter how good a place you are in. You are a very good friend, but heaven help those who upset you, because you do not forgive easily.

## WALNUT

You are a strange one. Mysterious and mystical you can be spontaneous to the point of totally confusing those who think they know you. Not everyone likes you but they all admire you. You are happiest on a one to one basis and will get jealous very easily. You can be a difficult partner but full of passion and warmth.

## WEEPING WILLOW

The nomad; a restless traveller who can ever be trapped or tamed. Alluring, drawing people to you, you can be demanding and capricious. You have great psychic energy and can feel your way through life seemingly smoothly. You may not want it, but you need a partner who can anchor you, or at least be a stable and unmoving rock for you.

If all this has whetted your appetite for communing with trees, then the following might be of interest to you. If you feel that you'd like to find a tree with really ancient knowledge, then these are places you should visit.

WILTSHIRE is the home of The Big Belly Oak – located in Savernake. It is eleven meters in girth and could be one thousand years old. It is said that if you dance naked, anti-clockwise around this tree at midnight, the Devil will appear to you.

Several venerable trees live in DEVON.

In Exeter there is the Heavitree Yew. Heavitree comes from the Old English for 'head tree' – heafod treow. A Head Tree is where the Saxon Kings used to hold their courts. This was because the impartial spirit of the tree would ensure fair hearings.

The Monkey Puzzle at Bicton is another Devonian giant. At twenty-six meters tall and four metres in girth, this is the largest Monkey Puzzle tree in England. There is a whole avenue of these green titans, brought as seeds from Chile in 1843.

DORSET has one tree of historical note.

The Tolpuddle Martyrs' Tree is a pollarded sycamore. The very first trade union was formed in the shade of this mighty tree in 1834, by, of course, the Tolpuddle Martyrs.

GLOUCESTERSHIRE has a giant coppiced lime tree. It has been carbon dated at more than two thousand years old, and is the oldest lime tree in Britain.

This county also has the most famous sweet chestnut in Britain. Named the Tortworth Chestnut, it is believed to have sprouted from a nut planted in 800AD. Many of its branches went on to root and so formed a tiny woodland – all from one tree.

HEREFORDSHIRE has another chestnut of repute.

The Spanish Chestnut, in the grounds of Croft Castle, Leominster, was grown from nuts salvaged from the Spanish Armada in 1592. It is said that the group of trees it stands within were originally planted in the formation of the Spanish Fleet.

SOMERSET has The Ashbrittle Yew. This three thousand year old tree is the largest in England. Thought to stand on a pre-Christian graveyard it is a massive twelve point two metres in girth.

In BRISTOL there is The Doomsday Oak. Probably this acorn's offspring was a mere stripling when its parent woodland was recorded in the Doomsday Book. At five hundred years old it's not the oldest oak my any means, but it has seen so much history that I'm sure it would respond to a hug.

# Appendix of fascinating facts

## GENERAL

A tree is a wonderful example of nature's engineering. No man-made edifice can match the way it forms and reforms itself to suit its surroundings and circumstances, while constantly remained totally self supporting in its structure, with no outside help at all.

Trees could be called the guardians of the planet, and are the key to its survival. They control the most vital element there is to human and animal life – water. They draw water from the ground in huge quantities and then return it to the atmosphere where it seeds clouds and causes the water to fall again as rain. This used to be considered solely the job of the oceans, but it has been discovered that trees play a major part in the process of water regeneration.

Trees are very complex entities, and much more like animals than you might think. Their intelligence, while different to man's, being hormone and chemically based, is nevertheless quite capable of analysing problems, and finding solutions. Trees that exist in windswept positions, for instance, will grow stronger and develop a wider base than trees in calm areas.

Trees evolve very quickly to adapt to situations, such as producing aerial roots that can process salt water, and creating barrel sized rain reservoirs in their trunks to store rainwater, in mainly dry areas. They also quickly form symbiotic relationships with other life forms, such as fungi to help them survive even on virtually bare rocks.

There are many reasons why tree shapes differ. A tree growing in poor soil may be stunted due to lack of nutrients, and a tree growing right next to an apartment building may have more leaves on the side facing the sun. Different kinds of trees have their own unique form, but the form that any tree has is also affected by the environment where it grows.

**Sunshine** and **water** are both essential for a tree to survive, and both influence tree *height, crown shape* (for example, a round treetop or the cone shape of a pine tree), and *the form of leaves.*

Some tree species grow quite tall and receive much sunlight. But what about those trees left in the shadows? Many trees collect sunlight that is filtered through the leaves of taller trees. These shaded *understory trees* survive by gathering indirect sunlight or sun flecks that break through openings in the canopy. A rounded crown seems to work best for gathering filtered, understory sunlight, which comes from many different directions.

The shape of the tree's crown also has a lot to do with where it lives. Nearer to the equator, the noontime sun is almost directly overhead all year. Tall trees with flat treetops (or crowns) are very common in this part of the world because the flat shape helps expose more of their leaves to the direct, overhead light.

Up nearer to the Arctic Circle, the sun is never directly overhead and is usually quite low in the sky. Trees in this part of the world tend to be cone-shaped (think of pine trees), with leaves from the top of the tree to the bottom, to make the most of this sunlight.

Finally, many of the trees up nearer to the Arctic Circle (like spruce, pines, and fir trees) have needles, partly because needles are especially adapted to cold, dry climates. Needles retain water better than broad-leafed trees like oaks and maples.

Mangrove trees are a natural protection for the land against the forces of a violent nature, such as Tsunamis. One has to ask the question as to whether the devastating events of 2004 would have been avoided if man had not removed the mangrove trees from the many of the coastal areas that were affected.

Physicist Ed Wagner discovered that if a tree is severed, the trees nearby although untouched, will put out an electrical pulse. This reaction happens within seconds, so Wagner theorises that it has to be something dramatic than electrical waves. It is an instant response, and doesn't seem to involve electromagnetic waves at all.

When attacked by parasites trees send out another signal that triggers other trees into with-holding nutrients from their leaves, so that they will be less palatable to the caterpillars or beetles that are about to spread to them from the damaged tree.

These inexplicable communications between trees has been verified in many experiments.

In other experiments the tiny scars on trees were analysed. These are nodules that form over the place where a branch was lost. They were found to contain chemicals and pollutants that were thus sealed away from the main tree and not allowed to enter it. Each old tree contains many of these nodules which are like tiny time capsules, and can be used to trace pollutants from the age at which they were formed. This means that nodules can be dated to eras such as the industrial revolution, when many previously unknown chemicals travelled through the air.

Yew trees have been on the planet since before the ice age. Among the longest living of all terrestrial trees, they are capable of standing for over four thousand years. The trees' ability to regenerate themselves, sometimes by aerial roots, makes them virtually immortal.

In a good year the oak tree will have many flowers, possibly up to several thousand. On an adult tree, so long as it has the right humidity, the right temperature, with no late frost in the spring, and sufficient rainfall in the summer, acorns will grow. They will mature to become full grown and ripe acorns by late summer. The chances of one acorn making it to become an oak tree are very slim; in fact they are less than 1/10,000. That means that for every 10,000 acorns, only one will become a tree.

All oaks were once protected by law. A man who felled or damaged one in Saxon times would be fined heavily. Further back, when oaks were considered sacred by Druids, every part of it was protected by fear of what the Gods might inflict on anyone who caused damage to an oak.

The word Druid is probably derived from the Gaelic word Duir, meaning 'oak'. Druid probably means 'men of oak'. They worshipped and performed rites in oak groves, which were not planted, but had grown naturally in circles. One of the Druid's most potent and much used plants is Mistletoe, and they believed it had been placed in the oak trees during lightning storms, as a sign from the Gods.

Ancient kings believed themselves to be the human personifications of the gods, and relied on this connection to bring them not only success in battle but also to bring rain to the land, thus ensuring fertility and a good harvest. These Kings placed crowns of oak leaves upon their heads, to show that they were from the Gods. Even in Roman times the successful leaders in battles were crowned with a circle of oak leaves. Oak leaves are still used today as decorative icons of military success.

Because oak trees live so long and grow so big, it was not unusual for individual specimens to have legends woven around them. The biggest tree in the parish was called the Gospel Oak, and this was where the Gospel was read out during the Beating of the Bounds ceremonies at Rogantide in spring.

There used to be an oak lined road leading to Glastonbury in Somerset, which was used as a processional route. Today only two of the giant oaks remain. Gog and Magog, which were named after the last male and female giants said to have roamed Britain.

In Sherwood Forest there is a venerable old tree which is said to be where Robin Hood and his Merry Men met to make their plans.

Oaks are actually members of the beech family, *Fagaceae*, and are long-lived, but slow-growing trees. The growth rate speeds up slightly as they reach their middle years, before slowing again. Oaks can commonly reach forty meters in height, although their average height is less in Scotland. They can easily reach fifty years of age and there have been reports of some that have been aged at over one thousand years. This is sometimes due to coppicing, which can extend the natural lifespan.

Oak trees can reach huge girth sizes, and some have even been twelve meters in circumference. With their spreading branches and domed crowns, they can sometimes be wider than they are tall. The 'pedunculate' oak usually has gnarled and twisting limbs, whereas the 'sessile' tend to be straighter. Because they are regular food for so many insects and other invertebrates, the leaves can become quite tattered looking by mid-summer, and will be full of holes. Because of this the oak does something quite unusual and often produces a second crop of fresh leaves, and interestingly, the official name for this phenomenon is Lammas growth. Lammas is the time of the Celtic festival of first fruits, which takes place on 1st August. During the autumn season the leaves turn yellow and brown because chlorophyll is withdrawn from them and this means the carotenoid pigments become visible instead. In sheltered, warmer regions the leaves can stay on the trees until December.

The British oak provides a habitat for more insects and other living organisms than any other tree. Because of its large size and longevity, it plays a unique role in forest ecosystems and many species have adapted to specifically live in tune with it.

A big oak tree can be home to over thirty-two species of mammal, sixty-eight species of bird, thirty-four species of butterfly, two hundred and seventy-one species of insect, one hundred and sixty-eight species of flower, ten species of fern and thirty-one species of fungi or lichen.

http://www.woodland-trust.org.uk/ancient-tree-forum/atfecology/ecology.htm

The larger the concentration of old trees in an area and the longer they have been present on site the richer the variety of species you will find among them.

Many of our rarest species associated with ancient trees only occur where there has been a continuous cover of old trees back through time on the site.

The older the tree the better the quality of wildlife associated with it over its lifespan but it is vital to have a good age structure of young to ancient trees on any site to maintain this wealth of wildlife.

There are literally thousands of species which depend on these features, and - because of the general scarcity of ancient trees in the countryside - a very high proportion of these species feature in lists of Red Data and Nationally Scarce species, ie our rarest and most threatened species. This is true right across Europe, not just in Britain. Indeed, in Britain we have a special responsibility as we not only have more ancient trees than most other European countries but also larger and more widespread populations of some of the special species.

The types of species are predominantly small and rather obscure -fungi, beetles, flies, lichens, and mosses, but also include cavity nesting and roosting species such as woodpeckers, owls and bats which are some of our most charismatic species of day and night.

The British landscape once dominated by wildwood after the last ice age has since Neolithic man been subject to constant change due to the management of land and the utilisation of its resources.

Existing countryside that was once extensive forest is now predominately a mosaic of agricultural, heath and moorland with woodland covering just some 11% of the land. Even the woodland has changed and just 2% of ancient woodland (woodland that has existed since 1600 and probably before) remains. It is very precious as it is the richest habitat in the UK. More recently farmland practices included the removal of hedgerows, hedgerow trees and many small woodland copses as a means of expanding field sizes and the converting pasture to arable, which usually included the removal of farmland trees, has furthered the decline of the tree in the British landscape.

Recent natural events have had a further profound impact on the landscape such as Dutch elm disease in the 1970s resulting in the death of the entire population of mature elms. The great storms of 1987 and 1990 continued to alter the treescape particularly in Southern areas with the loss of millions of trees. Throughout Europe further great winds such as the hurricanes of December 1999 are continuing perhaps with greater frequency to have dramatic effects on the treescape. At present, the current outbreak of oak dieback, which appears widespread throughout Europe, is causing the loss of many trees in some areas and environmental and pathogenic problems are threatening several other tree species such as alder and ash.

Despite all these events, fragments of the ancient treescape still remain today. Many of the surviving ancient trees can be found in the vestiges of the once extensive system of Royal Hunting forests and their successors, the more formalised medieval deer parks. More scattered groups of trees can also be found in historic parkland, wood pasture and ancient wooded commons with small groups and individual specimens to be found on farmland, village greens, churchyards and within the grounds of old historic buildings.

In the open countryside, scattered across much of England, ancient black poplars can be found on flood plains in meadows and occasionally in ancient hedges. Ancient ash cling to limestone rock in the Northern dales and in the Derbyshire dales coppiced lime stools are so old that the rock that they sit on has eroded away from their roots giving the appearance that the tree is supported by stilts. In the Scottish Borders ancient wood pasture oaks can be found at Cadzow and Dalkeith and ancient Scots pine survive in the Caledonian Forest way up in the Highlands. Wales has a history of hunting forests, a few of which were Royal Forests where occasional ancient trees can still be found. In addition old parkland oak trees survive in ancient parks such as Dinefwr Park and Chirk Park.

## Beliefs in Dyads or Tree Spirits

Trees are amongst the most amazing and most numerous organisms on the planet. For thousands, probably tens or hundreds of thousands of years, people have worshipped them, and talked to them. They are, after all, our original homes. Many people still do so today. It's something you can do too if you want to become part of the planet's communal soul.

Dryads are the 'higher Self' of trees and tree groups. Different trees have specific traits depending on the type of tree, the tree spirits vibrate on different levels, making them explicit to one particular space.

There are many more dryads in the countryside than there are within towns, because of this. Town noise and pollution and mechanical vibrations upset the natural energies and vibration of the tree spirits.

A dryad will operate, not by sight, as they have no eyes, but with what is almost like a 'range and detection apparatus' (RADAR). They take no notice of the human race except to find them an ever-increasing encroachment on their areas, disturbing the natural balance of things. However, those tree spirits that reside on ley lines can be friendly and helpful. Perhaps this is because they are more aware of us in these places of high energy connection.

It is said that if you can find two trees that have double trunks growing near each other, then between them you will find energy lines, and thereby a friendly dryad or two. Trees with violently twisted limbs that have been forced into a spiral shape, may be within an energy vortex, and here too you will find that the barrier between us and the spirit world can be crossed, making it possible to communicate with dryads.

Dryads have leapt and bypassed science by having cloning as their natural reproductive method. Like an amoeba, a tree spirit can reproduce by dividing a portion of itself into two. The new dryad will have duplication of all the original's memories and knowledge.

The ages of dryads vary and obviously the older the forest they dwell in the older the tree spirits there are likely to be. Some say that in a very privileged relationship with a dryad, it can be like having permanent and constant access to one's higher self.

You can even detect the presence of a tree spirit in an apparently dead piece of wood. If you are drawn to pick up such a piece and feel a pulse from it, then this is a special gift for you. Some people, needing a piece of wood will find a branch that has apparently fallen from a tree for no reason. This should be considered a gift.

### Celtic Tree Signs

Birch: December 24 – January 20

Rowan: January 21 – February 17

Ash: February 18 – March 17

Alder: March 18 – April 14

Willow: April 15 – May 12

Hawthorn: May 13 – June 9

Oak: June 10 – July 7

Holly: July 8 – August 4

Hazel: August 5 – September 1

Vine: September 2 – September 29

Ivy: September 30 – October 27, 2004

Reed: October 26 – November 24

Elder: November 25 – December 22

Nameless Day: December 23

There are many world breaking trees in the world. Most people would immediately correctly name the Californian Redwood tree (sequoia) as being the biggest. The very biggest of these giants even has its own name, 'General Sherman'. The General is 272 feet high and 35 feet in diameter, and is 109 round the base of the trunk. One single large redwood trunk would weigh up to 1400 tons, and would have the equivalent tonnage of cut timber as would be contained in several acres of normal trees. This weight would be the same as one of the Wicher Polish destroyers that served during WWII. It would also totally fill the cargo hold of the proposed new Boeing Pelican ULTRA (Large Transport Aircraft). The giant redwood tree is among the longest lived also. The oldest specimen, authenticated by ring count was almost 3200 years old.

The oldest known tree is the Ginkgo Biloba or Maidenhair Tree. It is the only tree survivor from the time of dinosaurs, which roamed the earth 135 to 210 million years ago. It is almost exactly the same in shape size and form as it was back then. A cross between a conifer and a fern, the tree reaches a very respectable 40 meters in height. Fossils of the tree have shown that 150,000 centuries ago they formed forests in the area now known as central Washington State.

One of the world's most famous trees must be Australian. Everyone knows the line about the 'jolly swagman' from Waltzing Matilda. The 'coolibah' tree mentioned in the song is actually another name for the Eucalyptus.

Specimens of the Australian Mountain Ash variety are among the tallest trees in the world and have been known to reach 92 meters in height. They are certainly the tallest flowering trees. Their big rivals, the redwoods, are of course conifers and as such don't have flowers.

Eucalypts have probably killed more people than any other tree, as they have a habit of suddenly dropping whole branches, without warning. Many a pioneer tree-feller was killed when a branch fell onto his tent after he had pitched camp below an overhang. For this reason the trees have the spookiest nick-name of all trees – 'the widow maker'.

**Fast Tree Facts to Consider!**

A healthy mature Birch tree can produce up to 1 million seeds in a good year.

The Seven Sisters oak tree in Lewisburg, Mandeville, Louisiana, is supposed to be the largest certified oak tree and it is estimated to be more than 1,000 years old.

Old Knobbly, is the oldest known British oak tree, being at least 400 years old. It lives in an area of woodland on Furze Hills, Mistley in Essex.

Tree fruits are always red, orange or yellow as these are the colours that birds prefer.
How did the trees know that?
The greatest reported depth to which a tree's roots have penetrated is 400 feet, and this was achieved by a Wild Fig tree at Echo Caves, near Ohrigstad, Mpumalanga, South Africa.

Two tonnes worth of tree timber has to be felled to make just one tonne of timber – we should be using hemp!

On average, each American uses more than 600 pounds of paper and almost 200 board feet of timber per year.

A whole aspen tree in Canada is chopped up to make a million matchsticks.

This website http://www.tree-register.org/ contains a unique record of Notable and Ancient Trees in Britain and Ireland.

In the UK, under the Town & Country Planning Act 1990, Local Planning Authorities (LPA) have specific powers to protect trees by making Tree Preservation Orders (TPOs). Under TPO legislation, it is an offence to cut down, top, lop, uproot, wilfully damage or wilfully destroy a protected tree without the written permission of the LPA. The legislation was revised in 1999 under The Town & Country Planning (Trees) Regulations 1999.

The coniferous forests of Northern Russia are the largest in the world. They cover 2.7 billion acres. The Siberian Larch is the most prolific tree in this forest and comprises 38% of the total.

The Amazon Basin has the largest tropical forest and 815 million acres.

Artificial Christmas trees will last for six years in your home, but for centuries in a landfill.

An acre of Christmas trees provides for the daily oxygen requirements of eighteen people.

Each year in the USA, the average yard tree cleans 330 pounds of carbon dioxide from the atmosphere through direct sequestration in the tree's wood and from reduced power plant emissions due to cooling energy savings.

In the USA each urban tree with a 50-year lifespan provides an estimated $273 a year in reduced costs for air conditioning, erosion control, storm-water control, air pollution, and wildlife shelter.

An average tree absorbs ten pounds of pollutants from the air each year, including four pounds of ozone and three pounds of particulates.

By slowing and filtering rain water as well as protecting aquifers and watersheds, trees improve water quality.

An Albizzia falcata in Sabah, Malaysia has been recorded as the fastest growing tree in the world. It grew 35 feet and 3 inches in 13 months, which is an approximate of 1.1 inches per day.

Conversely, the slowest growing tree is a White Cedar in the Great Lakes area of Canada is only 4 inches tall despite having lived for 155 years.

Rivalling the 'widow maker' of Australia, another tree can claim to be the world's most dangerous tree, with regard to poison. The Manchineel Tree of the Caribbean coast and the Florida Everglades secretes an exceptionally poisonous and acid sap. If it makes contact with your skin you can expect an immediate outbreak of blisters. If it gets into your eye, you could be blinded, and if you actually eat it, you will be at least very sick and possibly die.

In Japan people still believe that trees will sometimes sacrifice themselves to save people. In 1923 there was a massive earthquake and it is said that the trees which surrounded the houses in the area were destroyed by the quake in order to protect the houses. In 1991 a large cherry tree in the back garden of 10 Downing Street appeared to take the full force of the terrorist mortar bomb attack. If it hadn't been for the tree, the Cabinet Room and those in it would most likely have been destroyed instead

# O

is a symbol of the world,
of oneness and unity. O Books
explores the many paths of wholeness
and spiritual understanding which
different traditions have developed down
the ages. It aims to bring this knowledge
in accessible form, to a general readership,
providing practical spirituality to today's seekers.

For the full list of over 200 titles covering:

- CHILDREN'S PRAYER, NOVELTY AND GIFT BOOKS
- CHILDREN'S CHRISTIAN AND SPIRITUALITY
- CHRISTMAS AND EASTER
- RELIGION/PHILOSOPHY
- SCHOOL TITLES
- ANGELS/CHANNELLING
- HEALING/MEDITATION
- SELF-HELP/RELATIONSHIPS
- ASTROLOGY/NUMEROLOGY
- SPIRITUAL ENQUIRY
- CHRISTIANITY, EVANGELICAL
  AND LIBERAL/RADICAL
- CURRENT AFFAIRS
- HISTORY/BIOGRAPHY
- INSPIRATIONAL/DEVOTIONAL
- WORLD RELIGIONS/INTERFAITH
- BIOGRAPHY AND FICTION
- BIBLE AND REFERENCE
- SCIENCE/PSYCHOLOGY

Please visit our website,
**www.O-books.net**

# SOME RECENT O BOOKS

## The Barefoot Indian

Julia Heywood

Spiritual fiction, or not? Eternal wisdom is expressed in the context of modern day to day life, in a fresh, sensitive, intuitive, humorous and profoundly inspirational way.

1846940400 112pp £9.99 $19.95

## The Soulbane Illusion

Norman Jetmundsen

*Truly great writing...I was inspired. It is something I can recommend to anyone interested in the supernatural/thriller with a foundational faith to inspire people. If you like the works of C S Lewis, you will like this; if you like the works of John Grisham, you will like this. A good blend of the two.*
**Roundtable Review**

1903816599 308pp £7.99 $12.95

## The Soulbane Stratagem

Norman Jetmundsen

2nd printing

Listed by Wesley Owen as one of the all-time top 10 great Christian fiction titles.

*Rewarding, perhaps even life-changing; a readable, spiritually instructive work which should find a wide market.* **The Anniston Star**

*An engaging style of writing, an engrossing tale...truly exhilarating, a significant contribution to modern day theology.* **Birmingham Bar**

1903019699 296pp £6.99 $12.95

## Souls Don't Lie

Jenny Smedley

**A true story of past lives**

*People often go on about past lives they believe they've had, but rarely has anyone explained so eloquently and succinctly the art and science of using past-life regression to heal the life you're living now - a fascinating and recommended read.* **Barefoot Doctor**, healer and author.

1905047835 224pp **£11.99 $19.95**


## Torn Clouds

**A time-slip novel of reincarnation and romance, threaded through with the myths and magic of ancient Egypt.**

Judy Hall

*This is a great novel. It has suspense, drama, coincidence, and an extra helping of intrigue. I would recommend this literary marvel to anyone drawn to the magic, mystery and exotic elegance known as Egypt.* **Planet Starz**

1903816807 400pp **£9.99 $14.95**


## The Tree That Talked

Jenny Smedley

This is the story of an oak tree, from birth to death. Using the tree as our witness, we see many small moments in history-moments that rippled outward to affect the world. But the tree is more than a witness, it is connected to all the life around it. It, too, has its tragedies, its suffering, and times of renewal. After reading this, you won't think the same way about trees again.

1846940354 160pp **£10.99 $16.95**

# Daughters of the Earth

Cheryl Straffon

*Combines legend, landscape and women's ceremonies to create a wonderful mixture of Goddess experience in the present day. A feast of information, ideas, facts and visions.* **Kathy Jones**, co-founder of the Glastonbury Goddess Conference

1846940168 240pp **£11.99 $21.95**


# The Gods Within

## An interactive guide to archetypal therapy

Peter Lemesurier

*Whether you enjoy analyzing your family and friends or looking for ways to explain or excuse your own strengths and weaknesses, this book provides a whole new slant. It can be read just for fun, but there is an uncanny ring of truth to it. Peter Lemesurier combines scholarship with wry humour, a compulsive mixture.* **Anna Corser,** Physiotherapy Manager

1905047991 416pp **£14.99 $29.95**


# Maiden, Mother, Crone

## Voices of the Goddess

Claire Hamilton

*This is a vividly written and evocative series of stories in which Celtic goddesses speak in the first person about their lives and experiences. It enables the reader to reconnect with a neglected but resurgent tradition that is a part of the advent of the feminine in our time.* **Scientific and Medical Network Review**

1905047398 240pp **£12.99 $24.95**

## The Sacred Wheel of the Year

Tess Ward

*A spiritual handbook full of wisdom, grace and creativity. It dips into the deep wells of Celtic tradition and beyond to gather the clear water of life. This is a book of prayer to be treasured.* **Mike Riddell**, author of *The Sacred Journey*

1905047959 260pp £11.99 $24.95

## Savage Breast

**One man's search for the goddess**

Tim Ward

An epic, elegant, scholarly search for the goddess, weaving together travel, Greek mythology, and personal autobiographic relationships into a remarkable exploration of the Western World's culture and sexual history. It is also entertainingly human, as we listen and learn from this accomplished person and the challenging mate he wooed. If you ever travel to Greece, take Savage Breast along with you. **Harold Schulman**, Professor of Gynaecology at Winthrop University Hospital, and author of *An Intimate History of the Vagina.*

1905047584 400pp colour section +100 b/w photos £12.99 $19.95

## Tales of the Celtic Bards

With CD

Claire Hamilton

*An original and compelling retelling of some wonderful stories by an accomplished mistress of the bardic art. Unusual and refreshing, the book provides within its covers the variety and colour of a complete bardic festival.* **Ronald Hutton**, Professor of History

*Harp music perfectly complements the book in a most haunting way. A*

*perfect way in to the tales of "the Strange Ones".* **Wave**
1903816548 320pp with CD 230/152mm **£16.99 $24.95** cl.

## The Virgin and the Pentacle
### The Freemasonic plot to destroy the Church
Alan Butler

*The author unfolds the history of the tensions between Freemasonry and the Catholic Church, which he sees as reflecting that between patriarchal and matriarchal views of the godhead. It is essentially a power struggle that continues to this day. He makes a valuable contribution to the relationship between inner and outer history.* **Scientific and Medical Network Review**
1905047320 208pp 230/153mm **£12.99 $17.95** pb

## Way of the Druid
### The renaissance of a Celtic religion and its relevance for today
Graeme K. Talboys

*Enjoyable and revelatory...goes into closely argued debate on the nature of belief, religion and the Celtic metaphysic. Should be on library shelves-public and academic-and on the personal shelves of all those who already call themselves Druid.* **Liz Murray**, Liaison officer, Council of British Druid Orders
1905047231 304pp 230/153mm **£17.99 $29.95**